VISUAL QUICKSTART GUIDE

ADOBE
PHOTOSHOP ALBUM

FOR WINDOWS

Nolan Hester

 Peachpit Press

Visual QuickStart Guide
Adobe Photoshop Album for Windows
Nolan Hester

Peachpit Press
1249 Eighth Street
Berkeley, CA 94710
(800) 283-9444
(510) 524-2178
(510) 524-2221

Find us on the World Wide Web at: www.peachpit.com

To report errors, please send a note to errata@peachpit.com

Peachpit Press is a division of Pearson Education

Copyright © 2003 by Nolan Hester

Editor: Nancy Davis
Production Coordinator: David Van Ness
Composition: David Van Ness
Cover Design: The Visual Group
Cover Production: Nathalie Valette
Indexer: Emily Glossbrenner

ISBN: 0-321-19402-0

0 9 8 7 6 5 4 3 2 1

Printed and bound in the United States of America

To Mary, who brings color to my digital and analog worlds.

Special thanks to:
Nancy Davis, my editor nonpareil and her kids for doing their part;
David Van Ness, for turning these words and pictures into yet
another beautiful layout; Emily Glossbrenner, for always creating
indices that are not just accurate but smart; and Nancy Aldrich-
Ruenzel for making this life of at-home work possible. Home
wouldn't be home, of course, without Laika, who knows that twice
daily walks (or is it squirrels?) keep us both going. Thanks also to
the friends who so kindly let me use their wonderful photos: Amy
and Kelly Oliver, and Ray Montoya.

CONTENTS AT A GLANCE

TABLE OF CONTENTS

Introduction

Digital photography is fun. You click a button and the results appear on the camera screen almost instantly. Digital photography also can be frustrating. Anyone with a digital camera will instantly recognize this scene. Buried *somewhere* amid hundreds of computer files with names like 101-0144_IMG_2.JPG and 104-0459_STE.JPG are your pictures of Aunt Mutt and Uncle Leo at the Grand Canyon. Getting the pictures into the computer was easy. In fact, getting Uncle Leo to smile was a snap compared to trying to find that picture of him on your computer.

Relax. Adobe Photoshop Album, a new program, will make such hair-pulling searches a thing of the past. Not only will Photoshop Album easily find your photos, it also will inspire and guide you in creating online galleries, electronic greeting cards, and even printed albums. Instead of leaving your photos hidden in a shoebox, you'll be able to easily add them to email, store them as CD-based slideshows, or even order extra prints online that will make Uncle Leo grin all over again.

This book will help you master all the exciting options in Photoshop Album. It also will offer plenty of ideas and tips on how to organize, edit, and share your photos.

Hardware and Software Requirements

Anyone with a computer made in the past three or four years should have no problem running Photoshop Album.

To run Photoshop Album, you need:

◆ A Windows computer running at least the equivalent of a Pentium III processor chip with at least 128MB of RAM. (256MB is even better.)

◆ Your computer also needs a USB port. If your computer doesn't have one built in, you can add a PCI card with a USB port, which will let you connect your digital camera or a photo-card reader.

◆ A hard drive with at least 150MB of free space for installing Photoshop Album. Digital photos themselves can eat up a lot of space, though any computer sold in the past three or four years is likely to have plenty of space.

◆ A color monitor with at least a resolution of 800 x 600 and 256 colors.

◆ A CD or DVD drive for installing the Photoshop Album program.

◆ Microsoft Windows 98SE, 2000, Me, or XP.

◆ Microsoft Internet Explorer 5.0 or above.

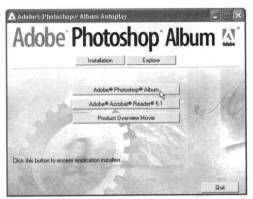

Figure i.1 When the installation screen appears, click *Adobe Photoshop Album*.

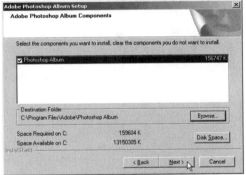

Figure i.2 By default, the program is installed at C:\Program Files\Adobe\Photoshop Album. Click *Browse* if you want to install it somewhere else.

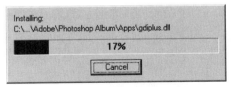

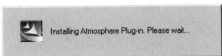

Figure i.3 A bar graph marks the installation's progress (top), along with separate dialog boxes for various program plug-ins (bottom).

Installing and Starting Photoshop Album

Like Photoshop Album itself, installing the program is fairly straightforward. Before you start, however, be sure to check the hardware and software requirements listed on the preceding page.

To install Photoshop Album:

1. Exit any other programs you may be running and insert the Photoshop Album CD into your CD or DVD drive.

2. Once the CD launches and the Adobe Welcome screen appears, click *Next,* choose your preferred language, and click *Accept* when the License Agreement appears.

3. When the installation window appears, click *Adobe Photoshop Album* (**Figure i.1**).

4. When the User Information dialog box appears, fill in your personal information and serial number, then click *Next.* (You'll find the serial number on the back of the CD case.)

5. By default, the installer offers to install the program at C:\Program Files\Adobe\ Photoshop Album. If you want to install the program elsewhere, click *Browse* and navigate to your preferred folder. Once you've picked a destination folder, click *Next* (**Figure i.2**).

6. The installation will begin, with a bar graph marking its progress (top, **Figure i.3**). A series of plug-in components also will be installed (bottom, **Figure i.3**).

(continued on next page)

7. The last installation dialog box gives you the choice of seeing the Readme file, which highlights details about running the program, and launching Photoshop Album itself. Make your choices and click *Finish* (**Figure i.4**). If you chose to start the program, the Photoshop Album startup screen will appear (**Figure i.5**), followed by the program's Quick Guide and main window. The next section, *Photoshop Album Basics* explains the Quick Guide, main window, and major tool bars.

To start Photoshop Album:

◆ Double-click the Adobe Photoshop Album shortcut icon on your desktop (left, **Figure i.6**) or use the Start menu to choose Programs\Adobe Photoshop Album (right, **Figure i.6**). By default, the Photoshop Album Quick Guide appears every time you launch the program; use it to start a task by clicking its icons and tabs. (See the *To turn the Quick Guide off or on* section on the next page if you want to work directly in the Photoshop Album main window.)

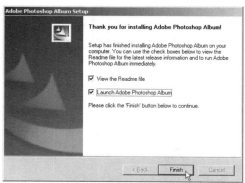

Figure i.4 Almost done: Check the boxes to make your choices and click *Finish*.

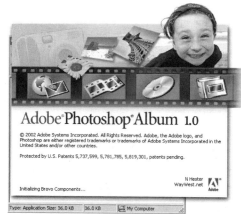

Figure i.5 When you chose to start the program, the Photoshop Album startup screen will appear.

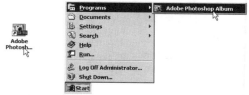

Figure i.6 To launch the program, double-click the shortcut icon on your desktop (left) or use the Start menu to choose Programs\Adobe Photoshop Album (right).

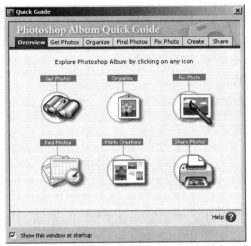

Figure i.7 By default, the Photoshop Album Quick Guide appears every time you launch the program.

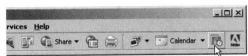

Figure i.8 To turn the Quick Guide off or on, click its icon at the far-right of the Shortcuts bar.

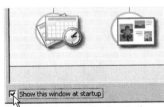

Figure i.9 Uncheck the box in the Quick Guide's lower-left corner if you do not want it to appear every time you launch Photoshop Album.

Photoshop Album Basics

Before you begin using the program, let's take a look at its main components. For more information on various aspects of the program, see the pages listed in each section.

The Quick Guide

By default, the Quick Guide appears every time you launch Photoshop Album. The guide's *Overview* tab (**Figure i.7**) invites you to click any one of six icons or matching tabs to perform common tasks. The icons and tabs correspond to Photoshop Album's six modes, which are explained a bit more later in the Introduction on page xx.

To turn the Quick Guide off or on

◆ At the far-right end of the Shortcuts bar, click the Quick Guide icon (**Figure i.8**). If the Quick Guide was visible, it will now disappear; if it was hidden, it will appear.

To hide the Quick Guide by default

◆ When the Quick Guide appears after starting Photoshop Album, uncheck the box in the lower-left corner (**Figure i.9**). The next time you launch Photoshop Album, the Quick Guide will be hidden by default.

THE QUICK GUIDE

The Main Window

The Photo Well dominates the program's main window (**Figure i.10**). It lets you toggle among various views, from tiny thumbnails to just a single large photo. Use the left-side Tags pane to organize and classify your photos using keywords. Photoshop Album makes it easy to customize the main window to show only what you need, when you need it. For more information about the Photo Well, see pages 20–22.

THE MAIN WINDOW

Menu bar

Shortcuts bar (next page)

Timeline (page 59)

Tags pane (page 32)

Tag tools

Tag categories (page 32)

Sub-categories for People tag

Search for tag (Amy & Kelly)

Tag categories applied to this photo

Tag's sub-category appears with cursor roll-over

Find bar with search criteria and results (page 55)

Photo Well

Video clip (page 24)

Scroll to move up/down in Photo Well

Photo's date & time

Selected photo; Double-click to view full size

Options bar (next page)

Status bar

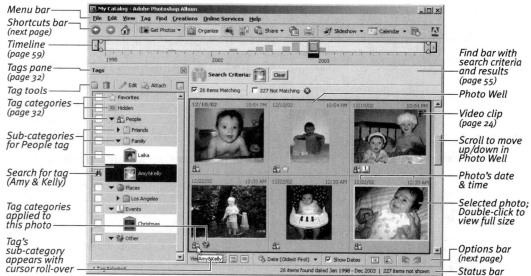

Figure i.10 The Photo Well, where you can toggle among thumbnail and close-up views of your photos, dominates the program's main window.

The Toolbars and Timeline

Using the Menu bar, Shortcuts bar, and the related timeline, you can perform most of Photoshop Album's major tasks. By clicking the icons in the Shortcuts bar (**Figure i.11**), you often can avoid hunting through the Menu bar's eight drop-down menus. Right below the Shortcuts bar lies the timeline, which you use to zero in on the photos you're seeking. Depending on how much information you need at the moment, the Options bar across the bottom of the main window can show or hide various views of the Photo Well (**Figure i.12**). For more information on the Find bar, see page 55.

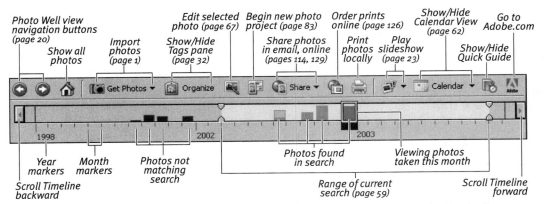

Figure i.11 The Shortcuts bar (top) provides quick access to all of Photoshop Album's major tasks. The timeline (bottom) helps you quickly find photos.

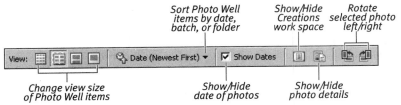

Figure i.12 Use the Options bar to change and sort views of the Photo Well, show or hide the Creations work space, and rotate selected photos.

Photoshop Album Modes

Photoshop Album has six modes, which are built around on the basic tasks you'll perform while working with your photos. Photoshop Album automatically switches from mode to mode, depending on which task you are performing. Click the Quick Guide's Get Photos tab, for example, and you're instantly working in the Get Photos mode. You can use the Quick Guide to walk you through any mode (**Figures i.13-18**), or perform a task directly just by choosing a menu command or Shortcuts icon.

Get Photos mode

Use the Get Photos mode to bring photos into Photoshop Album from a variety of image sources: a digital camera or memory card, a scanner, files already on your computer, or stored on CDs. For more information, see *Getting Photos* on page 1.

Organize mode

Organize mode goes to the heart of what makes Photoshop Album so powerful. By letting you create your own labels, or what it calls tags, Photoshop Album makes it easy to organize your photos in a variety of ways. You can create a general category tag, then break it down into as many sub-categories as needed. And Photoshop Album lets you apply multiple tags to the same photo, which means, for example, that you can apply enough labels to a shot to reflect that it shows your *mom* in the *garden* on the *Fourth of July*. For more information, see *Viewing and Organizing Photos* on page 19.

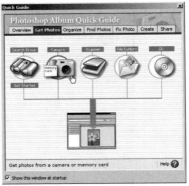

Figure i.13 Click the *Get Photos* tab and the Quick Guide will help you import photos from your camera or other sources.

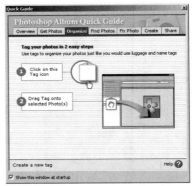

Figure i.14 Use the *Organize* tab to have the Quick Guide show you how to use tags to organize your photos.

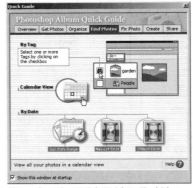

Figure i.15 The Quick Guide's *Find Photos* tab helps you search for photos by tag, calendar view, or by date.

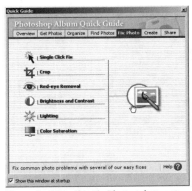

Figure i.16 Use the *Fix Photo* tab to get help correcting common photo problems.

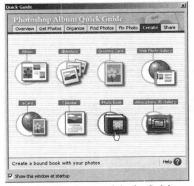

Figure i.17 The *Create* tab in the Quick Guide shows you how to create a variety of photo-based projects.

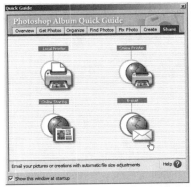

Figure i.18 The *Share* tab in the Quick Guide shows you how to print photos locally or using an online service. It also helps you create quick-to-download email versions.

Find Photos mode

Thanks to the amazing flexibility of the Find Photos mode, it doesn't matter what the file name is for an image. You can find it by searching for the tags you've applied to it or by when it was shot. The calendar view makes it easy to see how many, and on which days, photos have been imported into Photoshop Album. You can then flip through a day to find a particular photo (**Figure i.19**). Or you can use the timeline to set a range of dates to search (**Figure i.11**). For more information, see *Finding Photos* on page 55.

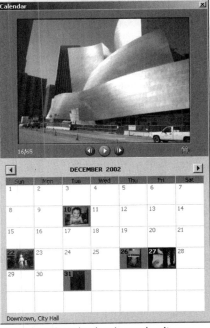

Figure i.19 The calendar view makes it easy to find photos for a particular date and then quickly review them.

Fix Photo mode

Even smart digital cameras make mistakes, not to mention the occasional photographer. The Fix Photo mode helps you quickly correct common problems with brightness and contrast, lighting, or red eye triggered by an indoor flash (**Figure i.20**). For more information, see *Editing Photos* on page 67.

Create mode

The Create mode takes your photos to a whole new level by helping you assemble an onscreen slide show, make a greeting card, or even publish a hardbound photo album. For more information, see *Creating Projects* on page 83.

Share mode

Half the fun of taking photos is sharing them with others. The Share mode makes it easy. For example, it can help you create a quick-to-download version of a photo to send through email (**Figure i.21**). At the same time, it will preserve your bigger original image file for later use in other projects. For more information, see *Emailing Photos* on page 114 and *Sharing Photos* on page 129.

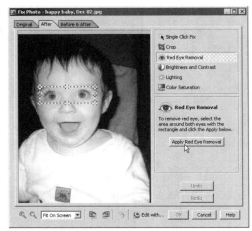

Figure i.20 The Fix Photo mode lets you correct common problems such as flash-related red eye.

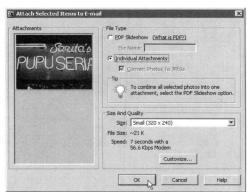

Figure i.21 Photoshop Album not only helps you create email-friendly photos but also tells you how long they will take to download.

Using this Book

The key to this book, like all of Peachpit's Visual QuickStart Guides, is that word *visual*. As much as possible, I've used illustrations with succinct captions to explain major functions and options in Photoshop Album. Ideally, you should be able to quickly locate what you need by scanning the page tabs, illustrations, and captions. Once you find a relevant topic, the text provides details and tips.

You'll find it easy to work your way through the book chapter by chapter. If you've got an immediate question about Photoshop Album, however, the book makes it easy for you to dive right in and get help quickly.

◆ **Tips:** Signified by a ✔ in the margin, tips highlight shortcuts for performing common tasks or ways you can use your new Photoshop Album skills to solve common problems.

◆ **Italic words:** When *italicized* words appear in the book's text, you'll find the very same words on the Photoshop Album screen itself when you reach that step in the program. The italicized term might appear as a button or tab label, the name of a text window or an option button in a dialog box, or as one of several choices in a drop-down menu. Whatever the context, the italics are meant to help you quickly find the item in what can sometimes be a crowded screen. If the step includes an accompanying illustration, use it to help you find the item being discussed. For example: Click the *Greeting Card* icon and the Workspace dialog box will appear.

(continued on next page)

◆ **Code font:** When a word or words appears in code font, it's used to indicate the literal text you need to type into Photoshop Album. For example: In the Find by Filename text window, type `friends` and press `Enter`.

◆ **Menu commands and keyboard shortcuts:** Menu-based commands are shown as: Edit > Update Thumbnail, which means click on the Edit menu and then choose Update Thumbnail from the choices that appear. Keyboard-based shortcuts (when available) are shown in parentheses after the first step in which they can be used. For example: (`Control``R`) means that you should press the `Control` and `R` keys at the same time to rotate a photo to the right.

◆ **Fades in figures:** Sometimes a Photoshop Album dialog box or menu is so deep that it can be hard to fit on the page with all the other figures and still leave it large enough to read. In those cases, I fade out the middle or end of the figure to save some space (**Figure i.22**). Nothing critical to understanding the step is ever left out. And it sure beats running teeny, tiny figures.

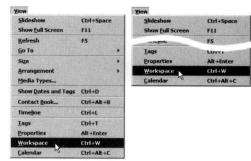

Figure i.22 Sometimes a deep original menu (left) or dialog box will be snipped in the middle (right) to save space on the printed page.

Updates and feedback

For Photoshop Album updates and patches, make a point of checking the Adobe Web site for Photoshop Album from time to time: www.adobe.com/products/photoshopalbum/

This book also has a companion Web site where you'll find examples from the book, and tips and tricks based on real-world tasks. So drop by www.waywest.net/psalbum/ when you can. You're also welcome to write me directly at psalbum@waywest.net with your own tips or—heaven forbid—any mistakes you may have spotted. Your help just might save Uncle Leo from some frustration when he buys his own digital camera—and the next edition of this book.

1

GETTING PHOTOS

To tap the powers of Photoshop Album, you start by importing your photos into the program. Photoshop Album can handle just about anything: brand-new digital camera shots, images stored on a CD or DVD, scans of prints or slides. It will even search your hard drive for image files you could never find on your own. One of the beauties of Photoshop Album is that it doesn't force you to actually copy all those non-camera images onto your hard drive. Instead, it creates a thumbnail or "proxy" image within a Photoshop Album catalog, which remembers where the original is stored. By using these proxy images, Photoshop Album is fast and easy to work with. When you edit the proxy image, those changes do not affect the original image, so your files—and memories—remain safe.

Setting Up Photo Importing

Photoshop Album can easily pull photos directly from your camera or a USB-enabled card reader. Once you set the camera or card reader import preference in Photoshop Album, that camera or card reader will be used by default for future photo imports.

To set the camera or card reader import preference:

1. Go ahead and plug the camera or card reader you'll be using into your computer's USB port, using the USB cable that came with the camera or card reader. If using a camera, turn it on after plugging it in.

2. Within Photoshop Album, choose Edit > Preferences (**Figure 1.1**) (Ctrl K).

3. When the Preferences dialog box appears, choose *Camera or Card Reader* in the left-hand list, then click the *Camera* drop-down menu in the right-hand panel (top, **Figure 1.2**).

4. Select your camera or card reader in the drop-down menu (bottom, **Figure 1.2**).

5. In most cases, leave the rest of the preference settings as they are (**Figure 1.3**), or see the *Camera or Card Reader Preferences* sidebar on page 3. Click *OK* to close the Preferences dialog box. You're ready to import camera or card reader photos into Photoshop Album.

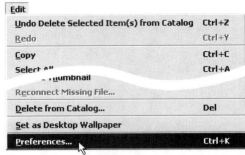

Figure 1.1 To set any of the preferences for importing photos, choose Edit > Preferences.

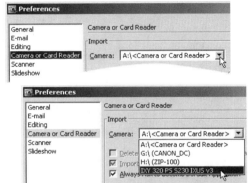

Figure 1.2 When the Preferences dialog box appears, choose *Camera or Card Reader* in the left-hand list (top), then select your camera or card reader in the drop-down menu (bottom).

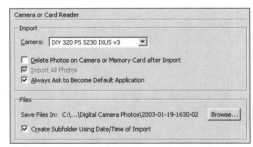

Figure 1.3 For more information on the rest of the preference settings, see the *Camera or Card Reader Preferences* sidebar.

Camera or Card Reader Preferences

Most of the Preferences dialog box's *Camera or Card Reader* settings should be left as you find them (**Figure 1.3**).

◆ **Delete Photos on Camera or Memory Card after Import.** By default, this is not checked, which means the photos will remain on your camera's memory card until you are sure they've been transferred to your computer.

◆ **Import All Photos.** If your camera supports WIA (Windows Image Acquisition) and you're running Windows XP or Windows Me, you'll be able to change the setting.

◆ **Always Ask to Become Default Application.** By default, this is checked and grants Photoshop Album permission to launch automatically whenever you connect a WIA-driven camera to a computer running Windows XP or Windows Me. Photoshop Album must be launched manually on computers running Windows 2000 or 98SE.

◆ **Save Files In.** By default, Photoshop Album stores images in a subfolder at `C:\Documents and Settings\My Pictures\Adobe\Digital Camera Photos\`. If you need to store them on a larger hard drive, click *Browse* and navigate to another folder.

◆ **Create Subfolder Using Date/Time of Import.** Checked by default, this option helps keeps the images folder a bit more organized in the rare event that you need to look in it directly.

Importing Photos from a Camera or Card Reader

How photos are imported into Photoshop Album depends on which version of Windows your computer uses. It's not something you need to mess with, however. Just install the software that came with your digital camera, and Photoshop Album will handle the necessary negotiations behind the scenes. In general, computers running Windows XP or Windows Me will use one type of software device driver (Windows Image Acquisition) for your camera, which will then automatically launch Photoshop Album whenever you connect your camera to the computer. Computers running Windows 2000 or Windows 98SE will install another type of device driver (TWAIN), which will require you to manually launch Photoshop Album.

Instead of importing photos directly from your camera, consider buying a memory card reader. Available for all the major memory card formats, such readers cost as little as $20 and offer several advantages over a camera-to-computer connection. Card readers, for example, do not need special software drivers to work. Plug the reader into your USB port and you're set. They also offer a shorter importing process similar to that used on Windows XP or Me computers—even if your computer's running Windows 2000 or 98SE. Using a card reader also saves your camera batteries. Digital cameras must be turned on for importing and many camera manufactures do not include a power cord, except as an expensive add-on. By using a card reader, you can save the camera's batteries for taking pictures.

To import photos directly from a camera:

1. Connect your camera to a USB cable and turn the camera on.

2. If you're running Windows XP or Me, Photoshop Album will launch automatically and begin the import process, so skip to step 7. If you're running Windows 2000 or 98SE, start Photoshop Album manually. Click the Quick Guide's *Get Photos* icon or tab and then click the *Camera* icon when it appears (**Figure 1.4**).

   or

   In the Shortcuts bar, choose Get Photos > From Camera or Card Reader (top, **Figure 1.5**).

   or

   From the Menu bar, choose File > Get Photos > From Camera or Card Reader (bottom, **Figure 1.5**) (Ctrl G).

3. If you set your camera as the default in *Setting Up Photo Importing* on page 2, it will be listed automatically in the Get Photos from Camera or Card Reader dialog box (**Figure 1.2**). If it's set for your card reader, use the *Camera* drop-down menu to choose your camera. Once you've made your choice, click *OK* to close the dialog box.

4. When the TWAIN dialog box appears, choose File > Connect to Camera (**Figure 1.6**). (The name of the dialog box will vary depending on your camera's driver.)

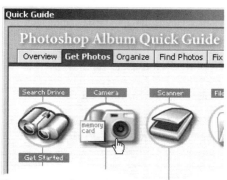

Figure 1.4 Use the Quick Guide to import photos from a camera by clicking the *Camera* icon under the *Get Photos* tab.

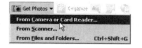

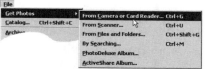

Figure 1.5 You also can import photos by using the Shortcuts bar to choose Get Photos > From Camera or Card Reader (top) or choose File > Get Photos > From Camera or Card Reader (bottom) (Ctrl G).

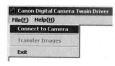

Figure 1.6 If you're running Windows 2000 or 98SE, Photoshop Album will launch the TWAIN dialog box. Choose File > Connect to Camera.

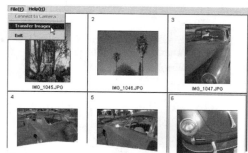

Figure 1.7 Click to select the photo you want to import (Shift-click to select more than one photo), and choose File > Transfer Images.

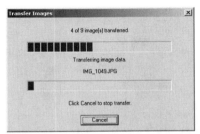

Figure 1.8 The Transfer Images dialog box tracks the transfer of the photos and then closes automatically.

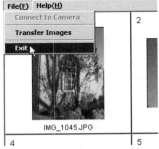

Figure 1.9 Close the TWAIN driver dialog box by choosing File > Exit.

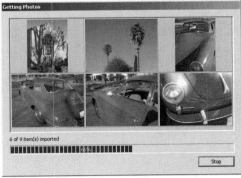

Figure 1.10 A status bar tracks the import of your photos into Photoshop Album.

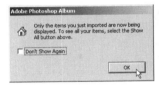

Figure 1.11 If you don't want to see this reminder after every import, select *Don't Show Again* and click *OK*.

5. When your photos appear in the TWAIN dialog box, click to select the photo you want to import ([Shift]-click to select more than one photo), and choose File > Transfer Images (**Figure 1.7**). The Transfer Images dialog box will display a status bar that tracks the transfer of the photos (**Figure 1.8**), and then close automatically when done.

6. Now close the TWAIN driver dialog box by choosing File > Exit (**Figure 1.9**).

7. The Getting Photos dialog box will appear with a status bar tracking the importing of the photos (**Figure 1.10**). Once the import is done, the dialog box will close automatically and an alert dialog box will remind you that Photoshop Album will display only the newly imported photos (**Figure 1.11**).

(continued on next page)

IMPORTING PHOTOS FROM A CAMERA

8. Click *OK* to close the alert dialog box (see the first *Tip* below) and Photoshop Album will display the newly imported photos in the Photo Well (**Figure 1.12**). You now can work with your new photos within Photoshop Album.

✔ Tips

■ After you read the alert dialog box that appears in step 7 (**Figure 1.11**), you probably don't need to see it again. Select the *Don't Show Again* checkbox before clicking *OK* and it will not reappear with each import.

■ If you forget to turn off your camera after importing photos, a reminder dialog box will appear (**Figure 1.13**). You can always click *Yes*, but your battery won't last as long.

■ To see all your photos, instead of just the new imports, click the Show All icon in the Shortcuts bar or press the Spacebar.

■ If you've already imported a photo, Photoshop Album will skip that photo during the current import session and alert you that it already exists in its catalog (**Figure 1.14**).

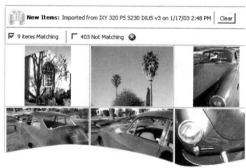

Figure 1.12 The newly imported photos will appear in the Photo Well where you can begin working with them.

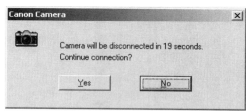

Figure 1.13 To save its battery, your camera will ask to shut down if left idle.

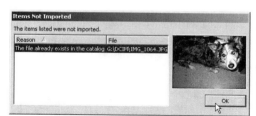

Figure 1.14 If you've already imported a photo, Photoshop Album will skip importing it and note that it already exists in the catalog.

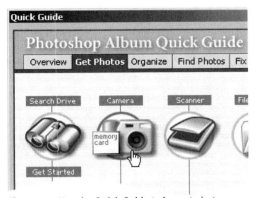

Figure 1.15 Use the Quick Guide to import photos from a card reader by clicking the *memory card* icon under the *Get Photos* tab.

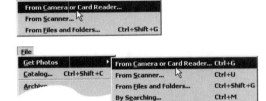

Figure 1.16 You also can import photos by using the Shortcuts bar to choose Get Photos > From Camera or Card Reader (top) or choose File > Get Photos > From Camera or Card Reader (bottom) (Ctrl)(G).

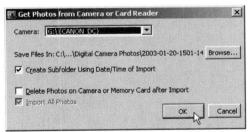

Figure 1.17 Make sure your card reader is selected in the *Camera* drop-down menu, then click *OK*.

To import photos from a card reader:

1. Connect your card reader to your computer's USB port or hub. The computer doesn't need to be turned off to do this. You only have to do this once since the reader can be left connected to the computer without interfering with other operations.

2. Start Photoshop Album. Click the Quick Guide's *Get Photos* icon or tab and then click the *memory card* icon when it appears (**Figure 1.15**).

   or

   In the Shortcuts bar, choose Get Photos > From Camera or Card Reader (top, **Figure 1.16**).

   or

   From the Menu bar, choose File > Get Photos > From Camera or Card Reader (bottom, **Figure 1.16**) ((Ctrl)(G)).

3. When the Get Photos from Camera or Card Reader dialog box appears, make sure your card reader is selected in the *Camera* drop-down menu, then click *OK* (**Figure 1.17**).

4. The Getting Photos dialog box will appear with a status bar that tracks the photos being imported. Once the import is done, the dialog box will close automatically and an alert dialog box will remind you that Photoshop Album will display only the newly imported photos.

5. Click *OK* to close the alert dialog box and Photoshop Album will display the newly imported photos in the Photo Well.

✔ Tip

■ Of the three options for importing, the Shortcuts bar icon is the most direct.

Importing from a Scanner

Photoshop Album can import images directly from a scanner—if it's connected to a USB port (and assuming you've installed all the software that came with your scanner). If you have an older scanner with a SCSI (Small Computer System Interface) connection, use the scanner to save the image to your hard drive and then import it into Photoshop Album following *Importing Files from Your Computer* on page 10. If you prefer to use the scanning program that came with your scanner, you can still bring the photos into Photoshop Album by following *Importing Files from Your Computer* on page 10.

To set scanning preferences:

1. Connect your scanner to your computer's USB port or hub and turn on the scanner. The computer doesn't need to be turned off to do this.

2. Start Photoshop Album and choose Edit > Preferences. When the Preferences dialog box appears, select *Scanner* in the left-hand pane (**Figure 1.18**). Photoshop Album should automatically list your scanner in the Scanner text field. If it does not, use the drop-down menu to find it in the list.

3. By default, Photoshop Album will save your scanner files as a *jpeg* file set to *Quality: 6 (Medium)*. If you expect to crop the photo by very much, however, you should change the setting to *Quality: 12 (Maximum)* (**Figure 1.19**). While your files will be larger—and take a bit longer to scan in—you will have more options when editing the photos and creating projects.

4. Once you've made your choices, click *OK* to close the Preferences dialog box. You're ready to start scanning.

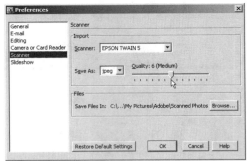

Figure 1.18 Use the Preferences dialog box to set your default scanner preferences.

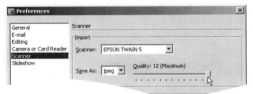

Figure 1.19 If you expect to crop the scanned photo by very much, change the setting to *Quality: 12 (Maximum)*.

A Tale of Two Formats

The JPEG format is superb for creating compact photo files that transmit quickly over email or the Web. But the drawback is that the JPEG format throws away data when it saves a photo. In fact, a JPEG image loses data *every* time you save it. If you repeatedly change, and then again save, a JPEG photo, its quality will decline a tiny bit with every save. In contrast, the TIFF format does not remove data, but it takes more storage space. If you expect to do a lot of editing on an image, import it as a TIFF file, make all your changes, and if you then want to send out an email or Web version, Photoshop Album can automatically convert it to the JPEG format.

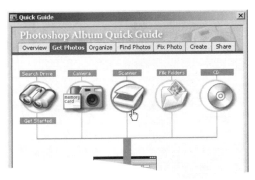

Figure 1.20 Use the Quick Guide to import photos from a scanner by clicking the *Scanner* icon under the *Get Photos* tab.

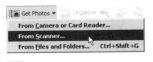

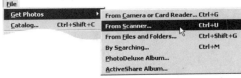

Figure 1.21 You also can import photos by using the Shortcuts bar to choose Get Photos > From Scanner (top) or choose File > Get Photos > From Scanner (bottom) (Ctrl U).

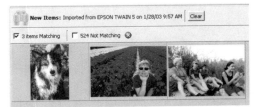

Figure 1.22 The newly scanned photos appear in the Photo Well.

To import photos from a scanner:

1. Connect your scanner to your computer's USB port or hub and turn on the scanner. The computer doesn't need to be turned off to do this. If you haven't already set the scanning preferences for Photoshop Album, see the previous page.

2. Click the Quick Guide's *Get Photos* icon or tab and then click the *Scanner* icon when it appears (**Figure 1.20**).

   or

   In the Shortcuts bar, choose Get Photos > From Scanner (top, **Figure 1.21**).

   or

   From the Menu bar, choose File > Get Photos > From Scanner (bottom, **Figure 1.21**) (Ctrl U).

3. If your computer is running Windows XP or Windows Me, skip to step 4. If it's running Windows 2000 or Windows 98SE, a dialog box for your scanner's TWAIN driver will appear and prepare to scan. Depending on your scanner (and whether you're scanning a print, film, or a slide), this may involve several steps and a series of automatically launching dialog boxes.

4. Depending on the size or number of images being scanned, the Photoshop Album Getting Photos dialog box will appear for only an instant, or for several seconds, with a status bar tracking the importing of the photos from the scanner. Once the import is done, the dialog box will close automatically and an alert dialog box will remind you that Photoshop Album will display only the newly imported photos (see the first *Tip* on page 6.).

5. Click *OK* to close the alert dialog box and Photoshop Album will display the newly imported photos in the Photo Well (**Figure 1.22**).

IMPORTING FROM A SCANNER

Importing Files from Your Computer

Photoshop Album offers two different ways to import photos already stored on your computer. If you have some specific files you want to import, Photoshop Album will let you navigate to them. But you also probably have lots of photos scattered across your hard drive that you'd rather not hunt down individually. In that case, Photoshop Album will search all your hard drives, present a list of what's found, and leave you the choice of bringing them into Photoshop Album. If you used Adobe's earlier PhotoDeluxe or ActiveShare programs to organize your photos, it's easy to import them right into Photoshop Album (see page 14). By the way, all these imported images will remain in their original location. Photoshop Album simply creates a proxy image in its catalog that points back to the original, enabling you to organize hundreds of already existing images from within Photoshop Album *without* needing a lot of hard drive space. If you ever move the original image, you'll need to find it when you use Photoshop Album to create a backup catalog. For more information, see page 47.

To import specific photos from your computer:

1. Click the Quick Guide's *Get Photos* icon or tab and then click the *File Folders* icon when it appears (**Figure 1.23**).

   or

   In the Shortcuts bar, choose Get Photos > From Files and Folders (top, **Figure 1.24**).

   or

   From the Menu bar, choose File > Get Photos > From Files and Folders (bottom, **Figure 1.24**) (Ctrl Shift G).

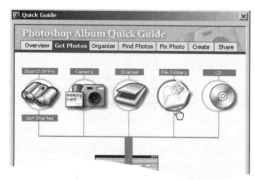

Figure 1.23 Use the Quick Guide to find specific photos on your computer by clicking the *File Folders* icon under the *Get Photos* tab.

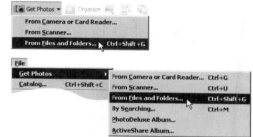

Figure 1.24 You also can find photos by using the Shortcuts bar to choose Get Photos > From Files and Folders (top) or choose File > Get Photos > From Files and Folders (Ctrl Shift G) (bottom).

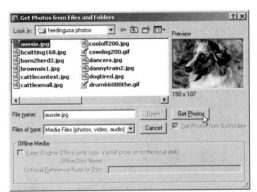

Figure 1.25 Navigate to the folder where your files reside, select them, and click *Get Photos* ([Shift]-click to select multiple files).

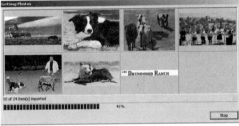

Figure 1.26 The Getting Photos dialog box displays the photos as they are imported from your hard drive.

2. When the Get Photos from Files and Folders dialog box appears, navigate to the folder where your files reside, select them, and click *Get Photos* (**Figure 1.25**). Use [Shift]-click to select more than one file.

3. The Getting Photos dialog box will appear with a status bar that tracks the photos being imported (**Figure 1.26**). Once the import is done, the dialog box will close automatically and an alert dialog box will remind you that Photoshop Album will display only the newly imported photos (see the first *Tip* on page 6).

4. Click *OK* to close the alert dialog box and Photoshop Album will display the newly imported photos in the Photo Well. You now can work with your new photos.

To search your computer for photos:

1. Click the Quick Guide's *Get Photos* icon or tab and then click the *Search Drive* icon when it appears (top, **Figure 1.27**).
   or
   From the Menu bar, choose File > Get Photos > By Searching (bottom, **Figure 1.27**) ([Ctrl][M]).

2. When the Get Photos By Searching for Folders dialog box appears, use the *Look In* drop-down menu to select which drives should be searched (**Figure 1.28**). Checked by default, the *Exclude System and Program Folders* and *Exclude Files Smaller Than* boxes ensure that you don't wind up grabbing thousands of irrelevant or tiny images. Make sure *Preview* is checked, then click *Search*. Depending on the size of the hard drive, it may take a minute or so to display the results, which will be listed by folder.

3. Choose a folder in the *Search Results* panel and the images it contains will be displayed in the right-hand *Preview* panel (**Figure 1.29**). Once you find the folder you want, ([Ctrl]-click to select multiple folders), click *Import Folders*.

4. The Getting Photos dialog box will appear with a status bar that tracks the photos being imported. Once the import is done, the dialog box will close automatically and an alert dialog box will remind you that Photoshop Album will display only the newly imported photos (see the first *Tip* on page 6).

5. Click *OK* to close the alert dialog box and Photoshop Album will display the newly imported photos in the Photo Well.

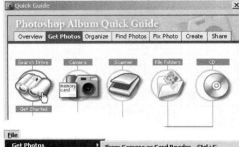
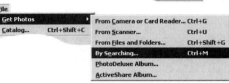

Figure 1.27 Search your computer for photos by clicking the Quick Guide's *Search Drive* icon under the *Get Photos* tab (top). Or choose File > Get Photos > By Searching ([Ctrl][M]) (bottom).

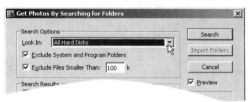

Figure 1.28 Use the *Look In* drop-down menu to select whether to search one or all your hard drives.

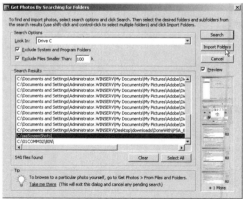

Figure 1.29 Choose a folder in the *Search Results* panel and its images will appear in the right-hand *Preview* panel.

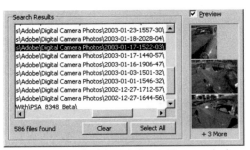

Figure 1.30 Not surprising: the hard drive search also finds all your Photoshop Album photos, which you don't want to import twice.

✔ Tips

- In general, you should not click the *Select All* button in the Get Photos By Searching for Folders dialog box unless you're searching a secondary hard drive free of application-related images. Otherwise, you'll wind up cluttering your Photoshop Album catalog with literally thousands of irrelevant images.

- Not surprisingly, the search will find all the photos you've already imported into Photoshop Album (**Figure 1.30**). You don't need to import them again, but if you forget and try anyway, Photoshop Album will display a reminder dialog box that you have already imported them.

Rights and Copyright

Just because a photo exists on your hard drive does not necessarily mean it's yours to use as you please. Many applications, for example, include tutorials, which often include copyrighted photos. If you're ever in doubt, don't add the photos to your Photoshop Album catalog or use them in Album-related projects. Photos emailed to you by friends are fine to use—if it's for private, non-commercial purposes such as posting a print on the fridge. If you're going to use them in something public like a book, however, be sure to get written permission first. (Again, my thanks to my friends for granting permission to use some wonderful photos emailed from around the globe. See page iv for credits.)

To import photos from PhotoDeluxe or ActiveShare albums:

1. From the Menu bar choose File > Get Photos > PhotoDeluxe Album or File > Get Photos > ActiveShare Album (**Figure 1.31**).

2. When the Finding PhotoDeluxe Albums or Finding ActiveShare Albums dialog box appears, click *Search* (**Figure 1.32**).

3. A list of the albums will appear in the Search Results panel. Once you find the album you want ([Ctrl]-click to select multiple albums), click *Import Album*.

4. The Getting Photos dialog box will appear with a status bar that tracks the photos being imported. Once the import is done, the dialog box will close automatically and an alert dialog box will remind you that Photoshop Album will display only the newly imported photos (see the first *Tip* on page 6).

5. Click *OK* to close the alert dialog box and Photoshop Album will display the newly imported photos in the Photo Well.

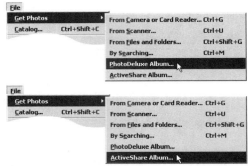

Figure 1.31 To import old PhotoDeluxe or ActiveShare albums, choose File > Get Photos > PhotoDeluxe Album (top) or File > Get Photos > ActiveShare Album (bottom).

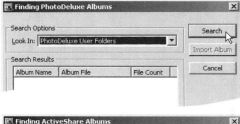

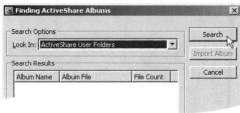

Figure 1.32 To find a PhotoDeluxe or ActiveShare album, click *Search*.

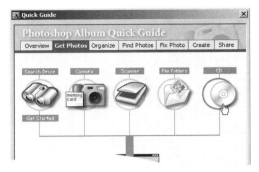

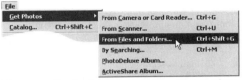

Figure 1.33 Use the Quick Guide to import photos from a CD by clicking the *CD* icon under the *Get Photos* tab. To import from a CD or DVD, choose File > Get Photos > From Files and Folders (Ctrl Shift G) (bottom).

Importing Photos from a CD or DVD

CDs and DVDs can easily store hundreds (or thousands) of images. When you're working with photos on these discs, Photoshop Album gives you the option of copying them to your hard drive, which potentially can take a lot of space, or simply creating proxy images that point back to the photo on the disc. When you want to edit the original, the proxy will help you find the CD or DVD where the original is stored. For more information on burning your photos to CDs or DVDs, see page 132. Obviously your computer must have a DVD drive to use DVDs.

To import photos from a CD or DVD:

1. Insert the CD or DVD into your computer's disc drive. If you're using a CD, you can click the Quick Guide's *Get Photos* icon or tab and then click the *CD* icon when it appears (top, **Figure 1.33**).

   or

   If you're using a CD or DVD, you can choose File > Get Photos > From Files and Folders (bottom, **Figure 1.33**) (Ctrl Shift G).

   (continued on next page)

2. When the Get Photos from Files and Folders dialog box appears, navigate to the disc folder where your images reside, select them ([Shift]-click to select more than one file), and click *Get Photos* (**Figure 1.34**). By default, Photoshop Album only searches for multimedia files. Use the *Files of type* drop-down menu if you want to search for other file types.

   or

   If you want to leave the original image on the disc and just create a thumbnail reference (also called a proxy), select *Keep Original Offline* (**Figure 1.35**). It's also a good idea to add information to the *Optional Reference Note for Disc* text field to help you find the original disc if you need to hunt it down later. When you're ready, click *Get Photos*.

3. The Getting Photos dialog box will appear with a status bar that tracks the photos being imported. Once the import is done, the dialog box will close automatically and an alert dialog box will remind you that Photoshop Album will display only the newly imported photos (see the first *Tip* on page 6).

4. Click *OK* to close the alert dialog box and Photoshop Album will display the newly imported photos in the Photo Well.

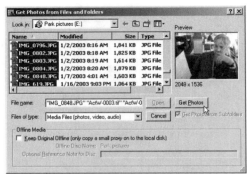

Figure 1.34 Navigate to the folder on the CD or DVD where your images reside, select them, and click *Get Photos*.

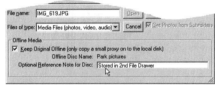

Figure 1.35 If you want to leave the original image on the disc and just create a thumbnail reference, select *Keep Original Offline*.

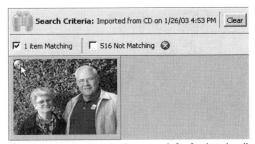

Figure 1.36 A disc icon in the upper left of a thumbnail image indicates that the original is stored on a disc.

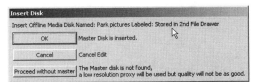

Figure 1.37 If you want to edit an image whose original is stored on a disc, Photoshop Album will display a note to help you find it.

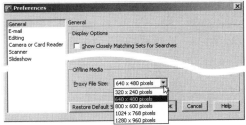

Figure 1.38 To create larger or smaller thumbnails, choose Edit > Preferences > General and make a choice in the Preferences dialog box's *Proxy File Size* drop-down menu.

✔ Tips

- If you selected *Keep Original Offline* in step 3, the imported thumbnail image will include a disc icon to indicate that the original is stored on a disc (**Figure 1.36**). If you want to edit the original image after you've put away the disc, Photoshop Album will help you find it using the note you added in step 3 (**Figure 1.37**).

- By default, Photoshop Album creates a 640-by-480 pixel thumbnail image for its catalog. That's big enough to see without taking up too much space. If you want Photoshop Album to create larger or smaller thumbnails, choose Edit > Preferences > General and use the Preferences dialog box's *Proxy File Size* drop-down menu to choose another default (**Figure 1.38**). Once you make your choice, click *OK* to close the dialog box.

Deleting Photos from Photoshop Album

Given the itty-bitty screens on most digital cameras, you may not be able to tell if a photo is worth keeping until after you import it into Photoshop Album. Lots of photo problems, such as red eye, can be fixed. Fuzzy focus, foolish expressions, accidental shots of the sky—you're better off deleting them now. That way you can concentrate on working with all the great shots you did get.

To delete photos from Photoshop Album:

1. Within the Photo Well, click on any image you want to delete ([Ctrl]-click to select multiple images). The selected items will be surrounded with a bright yellow border.

2. Press [Delete] and when the Confirm Deletion from Catalog dialog box appears (**Figure 1.39**), you have two choices: Click *OK* immediately to delete just the thumbnail (proxy) image from the Photoshop Album catalog. Or select *Also delete selected item(s) from the hard disk* and then click *OK* to remove the original image from your computer as well.

✔ Tip

■ Making the right choice in step 2 boils down to this: If you imported the image directly into Photoshop Album and decide you don't want to use it, then you'll probably also want to remove the original from your hard drive. But if the image already existed on your computer for some other use, then just click *OK*—leaving the original but removing the Photoshop Album thumbnail.

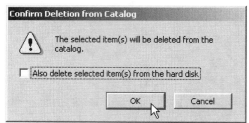

Figure 1.39 When you try to delete an image, a warning dialog box offers you the choice of deleting just the thumbnail or the original as well.

VIEWING AND ORGANIZING PHOTOS

2

This chapter covers three tools for organizing your photos: captions and notes, tags, and catalogs. Each has a different role. Use captions and notes to add details about specific photos. Tags are used to label groups of photos that have things in common. Photoshop Album also uses what it calls catalogs (in-the-background multimedia databases) as a way of tracking all your photos.

Most of your captions will inevitably contain unique descriptions that can help you find a single photo among hundreds of images. In contrast, the tags you create should apply to broad recurring categories. While "Jodi wins baseball championship" makes a great caption for a few photos, it's too specific for a tag—unless you have 30–40 photos of that game. "Little League" or "Family-Jodi" might be examples of a more useful tag. Tags don't tell you much about individual photos, but they do help you find a group of photos likely to contain the one photo you want to see. For more information on captions, see page 27. For more information on tags, see page 32.

Most of the time you won't even need to think about catalogs. Making regular backups of your catalogs, however, is essential for protecting your photos should anything go wrong. For more information on catalogs, see page 46.

Working with Photos

The Photo Well lets you vary your view of the photos, depending on your task. For a quick overview of recently imported photos, the smallest thumbnail view may be the most useful (**Figure 2.1**). If you're inspecting photos to see which need editing or cropping, the single-photo view works best (**Figure 2.2**). If you want to see a selection of photos in a full-screen sequence, Photoshop Album includes what it calls an instant slideshow. You can't reorder the sequence, but it lets you get a quick sense of how the photos look. You also can view any of your video clips directly in the Photo Well.

Ways to change photo sizes in the Photo Well:

◆ Click any of the four *View* icons at the bottom-left of the Options bar (top, **Figure 2.3**).

◆ Choose View > Size and make a choice from the submenu (bottom, **Figure 2.3**).

◆ Use the keyboard commands:
Ctrl 0 for the small thumbnail view,
Ctrl 1 for the medium thumbnail view,
Ctrl 2 for the large thumbnail view, or
Ctrl 3 for the single photo view.

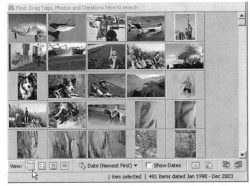

Figure 2.1 To see as many photos as possible in the Photo Well, use the smallest thumbnail view.

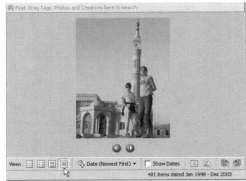

Figure 2.2 The single-photo view works best for inspecting photos that might need editing or cropping.

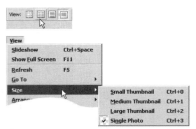

Figure 2.3 To change photo sizes in the Photo Well, click one of the *View* icons in the Options bar (top), or choose View > Size and make a choice from the submenu (bottom).

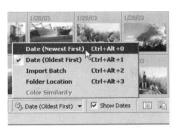

Figure 2.4 To rearrange the Photo Well view, click the arrangement menu in the Options bar.

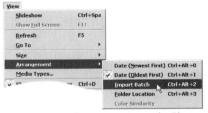

Figure 2.5 You also can rearrange the Photo Well view by choosing View > Arrangement and making a choice from the drop-down menu.

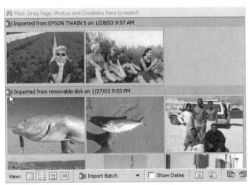

Figure 2.6 The film roll icon shows that these photos were imported into Photoshop Album at the same time.

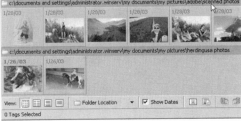

Figure 2.7 The folder icon shows that these photos are all stored in the same place.

To rearrange the Photo Well view:

◆ Click the Photo Well arrangement menu in the Options bar and make a choice from the pop-up menu (**Figure 2.4**).

◆ From the Menu bar, choose View > Arrangement and make a choice from the drop-down menu (**Figure 2.5**).

◆ Use the keyboard commands (**Figure 2.5**): Ctrl Alt 0 to see the newest photos first, Ctrl Alt 1 to arrange with the oldest first, Ctrl Alt 2 to see by import batch (**Figure 2.6**), or Ctrl Alt 3 to see based on folder location (**Figure 2.7**).

(continued on next page)

REARRANGING THE PHOTO WELL VIEW

✔ Tips

- Arranging the Photo Well with the newest photos first will let you quickly find your freshest photos. By default, the Photo Well is arranged with the oldest photos at the top, which puts the photos you just imported out of sight at the bottom of the well.

- By default, *Show Dates* is checked in the Options bar. To hide the date—and fit more photos into the Photo Well— uncheck *Show Dates* (**Figure 2.8**). Just remember that hiding the dates also will hide tag icons.

- In both **Figure 2.4** and **Figure 2.5**, the *Color Similarity* choice is grayed out. For more information on this powerful option, see *Finding Photos of Similar Color* on page 66.

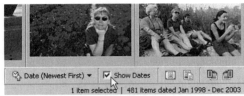

Figure 2.8 To hide the date—and fit more photos into the Photo Well—uncheck *Show Dates*.

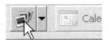

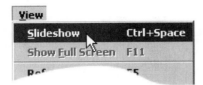

Figure 2.9 To view an instant slideshow, click the Slideshow icon (top) or choose View > Slideshow (bottom).

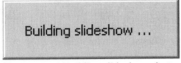

Figure 2.10 A Building slideshow alert box will appear while Photoshop Album assembles the photos.

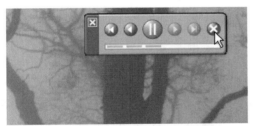

Figure 2.11 A mini-control panel will appear in the screen's upper right, which you can use to move through or stop the slideshow.

To view an instant slideshow:

1. In the Photo Well, select the photos you want to see in a full-screen instant slideshow. ([Shift]-click to select adjacent photos or [Ctrl]-click to select non-adjacent photos.)

2. In the Shortcuts bar, click the Slideshow icon or from the Menu bar, choose View > Slideshow ([Ctrl]-Spacebar) (**Figure 2.9**). A Building slideshow alert box will appear while Photoshop Album assembles the photos into a slideshow (**Figure 2.10**). The photos will then appear full-screen. A mini-control panel will appear in the screen's upper right, which you can use to move through or stop the slideshow (**Figure 2.11**). Click anywhere on the screen to return to the Photoshop Album Photo Well.

✔ Tip

- Such instant slideshows display photos in the order they appear in the Photo Well, and you cannot change that order. To create a slideshow with the photos shown in a particular order, see *Creating Slideshows* on page 94.

VIEWING AN INSTANT SLIDESHOW

To play a video clip:

◆ In the Photo Well, double-click the video clip you want to see (**Figure 2.12**). When the video clip window appears, click the big center play button (**Figure 2.13**). Click the X icon to close the video window and return to the Photo Well.

✔ Tip

■ The Photoshop Album Creations Wizard can help you create video CDs; see *Creating Projects* on page 83.

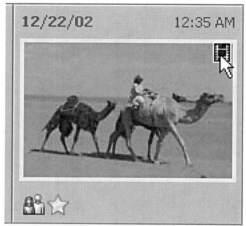

Figure 2.12 To play a video clip (marked by a film strip icon in the upper right), just double-click it.

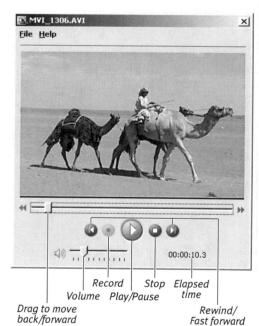

Record   Stop   Elapsed
Volume   Play/Pause   time

Drag to move
back/forward
                                    Rewind/
                                    Fast forward

Figure 2.13 Click the big center play button to start a video clip.

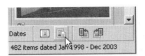

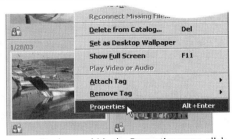

Figure 2.14 To show or hide the Properties pane, click the Show/Hide Properties icon in the Options bar (top), or right-click a photo and choose Properties from the pop-up menu (bottom).

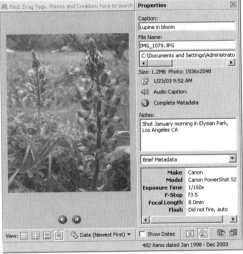

Figure 2.15 Use the Properties pane to add captions, notes, and even audio captions to a photo.

Viewing, Adding or Changing Photo Details

The Properties pane is where you'll add much of the information that helps flesh out the details of a photo. By adding captions, notes, and even audio captions to a photo you preserve details that make viewing your photos even more fun. You can add such details whenever you have time or just before you create a slideshow or photo book. For more information on slideshows and other Photoshop Album projects, see page 83. Photoshop Album also automatically captures a bunch of details about your digital camera's exposures, called metadata, which can be very helpful to understand why some photos look great.

Ways to show or hide the Properties pane:

◆ Click the Show/Hide Properties icon in the Options bar (top, **Figure 2.14**), or from the Menu bar, choose View > Properties ([Alt][Enter]). The Properties pane will appear down the right side of the Photo Well (**Figure 2.15**).

◆ Right-click any photo in the Photo Well and from the pop-up menu choose Properties (bottom, **Figure 2.14**). The Properties pane will appear down the right side of the Photo Well (**Figure 2.15**).

VIEWING, ADDING OR CHANGING PHOTO DETAILS

To show or hide a photo's metadata:

◆ To open the metadata for a photo, make sure the Properties pane is visible, then click the *Complete Metadata* icon in the Properties pane. The Complete Metadata window will appear (**Figure 2.16**).

◆ To close the Complete Metadata window, click the X icon in the window's upper-right corner. The window will close.

✔ Tip

■ While all that metadata captured from your digital camera might seem a bit exotic, you'll find it immensely helpful as you begin editing photos and want to understand why certain photos turn out better than others.

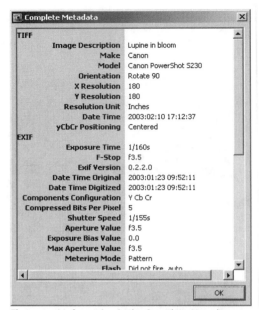

Figure 2.16 Information in the Complete Metadata window can be very helpful in understanding why certain photos turn out better than others.

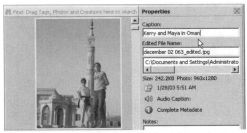

Figure 2.17 If the Properties pane is visible, select a photo in the Photo Well, and you can type the caption directly in the *Caption* text window.

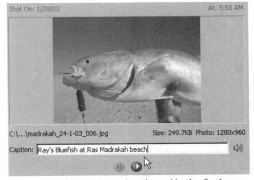

Figure 2.18 If *Show Dates* is selected in the Options bar, double-click any thumbnail and it will appear as a single photo with a *Caption* text window.

To add a photo caption:

◆ If you're working in any view other than single photo and the Properties pane is visible, select a photo in the Photo Well, and you can type the caption directly in the Properties pane's *Caption* text window (**Figure 2.17**).

or

◆ If *Show Dates* is selected in the Options bar, you can double-click any thumbnail photo in the Photo Well and it will appear as a single photo with a *Caption* text window (**Figure 2.18**). You can then type in your caption information.

✔ Tips

■ If you're working in the single photo view, you can quickly move to another photo by clicking the forward or back button just below the *Caption* text window.

■ A caption can be no longer than 63 characters—about equal to this section's introduction.

To remove a photo caption:

1. Select one or more photos in the Photo Well (Shift-click to select adjacent photos; Ctrl-click to select non-adjacent photos).

2. From the Menu bar, choose Edit > Clear Caption or Edit > Clear Captions of Selected Items. The captions will be removed from the selected photos.

To add a note to a photo:

◆ Make sure the Properties pane is visible, select a photo in the Photo Well, and type in the Properties pane's *Notes* text field.

✔ Tip

■ You can type up to 1,023 characters in a note, which allows you to add a fair amount of detail.

ADDING, REMOVING A PHOTO CAPTION OR NOTE

To add an audio caption:

1. Make sure the Properties pane is visible, select a photo in the Photo Well, and click the *Audio Caption* icon in the Properties pane (**Figure 2.19**).

2. When the Select Audio File dialog box appears, choose File > Browse if there's an audio file already on your computer that you want to attach to the photo (**Figure 2.20**). Use the Specify Audio File dialog box to navigate to the desired file and then open it (**Figure 2.21**). (See the *Tip* on where you can find some audio files that came with Photoshop Album.)

   If you want to attach some spoken notes to the photo, make sure your USB-enabled microphone is attached and click the red record button to start recording (**Figure 2.22**). When you're done and want to stop recording, click the record button again.

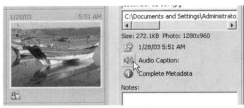

Figure 2.19 Click the *Audio Caption* icon in the Properties pane to add an audio caption.

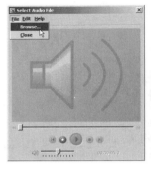

Figure 2.20 When the Select Audio File dialog box appears, choose File > Browse to navigate to an audio file already on your computer.

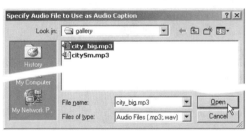

Figure 2.21 Use the Specify Audio File dialog box to navigate to the desired file and open it.

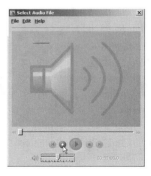

Figure 2.22 To attach spoken notes to a photo, make sure your USB-enabled microphone is attached and click the record button to start recording.

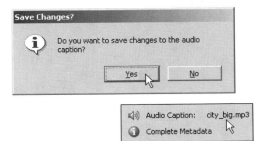

Figure 2.23 After finding or creating an audio file, click *Yes* to save it (top), and it will then appear in the Properties pane (bottom).

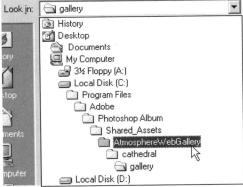

Figure 2.24 Here's where to find audio files if you want to experiment with the audio caption feature.

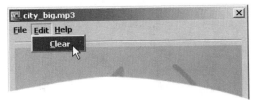

Figure 2.25 To remove an audio caption from a photo, choose Edit > Clear.

3. Once you've found or made an audio clip for the photo, close the Select Audio File dialog box by clicking the X icon in the upper right, and when the Save Changes dialog box appears, click *Yes* (top, **Figure 2.23**). The name of the attached audio file will appear in the Properties pane next to the Audio Caption icon (bottom, **Figure 2.23**).

✔ Tip

- If you want to experiment with the audio caption feature but don't have any appropriate files on your computer, navigate to: /PhotoshopAlbum/Shared_Assets/ AtmosphereWebGallery/ and look in any of the enclosed folders (**Figure 2.24**).

To remove an audio caption:

1. Click the Audio Caption button in the Properties pane and when the Select Audio File dialog box appears, choose Edit > Clear (**Figure 2.25**).

2. When the Save Changes dialog box appears, click *Yes* (top, **Figure 2.23**). The name of the attached audio file will no longer appear in the Properties pane next to the Audio Caption button.

To rename a photo:

1. Select the photo in the Photo Well and from the Menu bar, choose File > Rename.

2. When the Rename dialog box appears, type in the New Name text window and click OK. The name of the file will be changed.

✔ Tip

■ Though you may occasionally want to rename a particular photo, resist with all your might the temptation to do this. The reason? Photoshop Album was designed to make it unnecessary to worry about what a digital photo might be named. If you start renaming files just for the sake of tidiness, you'll be missing the real fun of having digital photos, which is to create cool projects with them.

Source Dictates Date and Time

The date and time displayed for a photo will vary depending on the photo's original source. If you imported the photo from a digital camera or a card reader, the date and time reflects the time the photo was taken (assuming the camera's clock is set properly). If you import a photo from a CD or a file already on your computer, the date and time reflects when the file was first created. Photos from a scanner show the date and time when the image was imported into Photoshop Album. If all your digital camera photos are off by 12 hours (showing 2 a.m. when it should be 2 p.m., for example), recheck your camera's clock setting. If you need to change the date or time for photos already in Photoshop Album, see the next page.

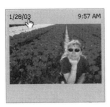

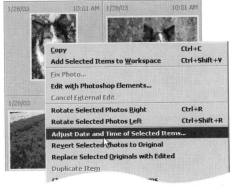

Figure 2.26 Click the date or time above the selected photo (top) or right-click and choose Adjust Date and Time of Selected Items (bottom).

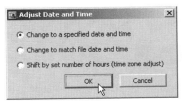

Figure 2.27 Use the Adjust Date and Time dialog box to change the date, time, or shift the time zone.

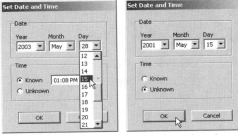

Figure 2.28 Use the *Year*, *Month*, and *Day* drop-down menus to change the settings (left), or select *Unknown* if you don't know when the photo was taken (right).

To change a photo's date or time:

1. Make sure *Show Dates* is selected in the Options bar at the bottom of the Photo Well. Click to select a photo within the Photo Well (Shift-click adjacent photos or Ctrl-click non-adjacent photos).

2. Within the Photo Well, click the date or time stamp above the selected photo(s) (top, **Figure 2.26**) or right-click and choose *Adjust Date and Time of Selected Items* from the drop-down menu (bottom, **Figure 2.26**).

3. When the Adjust Date and Time dialog box appears, *Change to a specified date and time* will be selected by default (**Figure 2.27**). The second choice lets you reset the date and time of when the photo was first imported into Photoshop Album, while the last choice lets you quickly shift, for example, from 1 a.m. to 1 p.m. Make your choice and click *OK*.

4. When the Set Date and Time dialog box appears, use the *Year*, *Month*, and *Day* drop-down menus to change the settings (left, **Figure 2.28**). Within the *Time* panel, use the arrows on the right side of the *Known* text field. If you don't know what time the photo was shot—or don't want to specify that—select Unknown. Click *OK* when you're done (right, **Figure 2.28**). The selected photo(s) in the Photo Well will reflect the date and time changes (**Figure 2.29**).

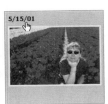

Figure 2.29 The new date will appear above the photo in the Photo Well.

Working with Tags

Before Photoshop Album came along, you often faced a quandary when organizing and filing your prints and slides. Should you arrange them by date, by trip, by subject? Using Photoshop Album tags, you don't have to choose. With tags, you can quickly file your photo prints in multiple ways—without reshuffling the photos themselves. Remember: Tags don't actually change your photos. Instead Photoshop Album stores the tag information in the behind-the-scenes catalog.

To show or hide the Tags pane:

◆ In the Shortcuts bar, click the *Organize* icon (top, **Figure 2.30**) and the Tags pane will appear (**Figure 2.31**).

◆ In the Menu bar, choose View > Tags (bottom, **Figure 2.30**) and the Tags pane will appear (**Figure 2.31**).

✔ Tip

■ You also can close the Tags pane by clicking the close window icon above the Tags toolbar (**Figure 2.32**).

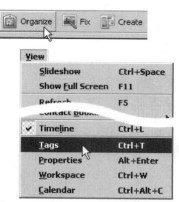

Figure 2.30 To show or hide the Tags pane, click the *Organize* icon (top) or choose View > Tags (bottom).

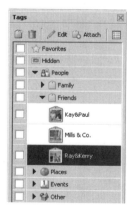

Figure 2.31 The Tags pane makes it easy to add, remove, change, or rearrange tags.

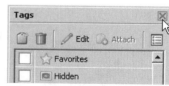

Figure 2.32 You can close the Tags pane by clicking the close window icon above the Tags toolbar.

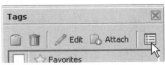

Figure 2.33 Click the far-right icon in the Tags toolbar to change the display size for tags.

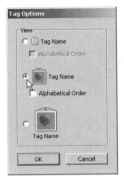

Figure 2.34 By default, the middle choice is selected in the Tag Options dialog box.

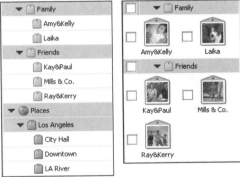

Figure 2.35 Two other tag display options: smaller tags without photos (left) or tags with even larger photos (right).

To change the Tags pane view:

1. With the Tags pane visible, click the far-right icon in the Tags toolbar (**Figure 2.33**). When the Tag Options dialog box appears, the middle choice is selected by default (**Figure 2.34**).

2. Select the top choice to display smaller tags without photos, or the bottom choice to use tags with even larger photos (**Figure 2.35**). Click *OK* to close the Tag Options dialog box and the Tags pane will reflect the change.

To create a new tag:

1. With the Tags pane visible, click the first icon in the Tags toolbar (top, **Figure 2.36**) or choose Tag > New Tag ([Ctrl][N]) (bottom, **Figure 2.36**).

2. When the Tag Editor dialog box appears, choose a *Category* (or a sub-category if you've created any) using the drop-down menu (left, **Figure 2.37**). For more information on creating sub-categories and organizing tags, see page 42–43.

3. Use the *Tag Name* text window to give your tag a short but descriptive name, add any needed extra information in the *Note* field, then click *OK* (right, **Figure 2.37**). The dialog box will close and the new tag will appear in the Tags pane under the assigned category or sub-category (**Figure 2.38**).

✔ Tips

■ The icon for the new tag will remain *?* until you attach it to a photo.

■ In step 1, if you first click on a particular tag category or sub-category, Photoshop Album will automatically assign your tag to that category (**Figure 2.39**).

■ You also can create a new tag within a particular category or sub-category by right-clicking on it and then using the drop-down menu to choose Create new tag in [name of] sub-category (**Figure 2.40**).

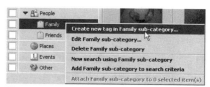

Figure 2.40 By right-clicking a tag, you can create a new tag within that category or sub-category.

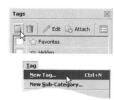

Figure 2.36 To create a new tag, click the first icon in the Tags toolbar (top) or choose Tag > New Tag (bottom).

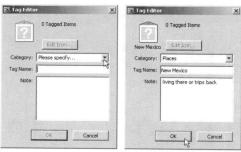

Figure 2.37 Choose a *Category* (or a sub-category if you've created any) using the drop-down menu (left), then give your tag a name and add extra information in the *Note* text window (right).

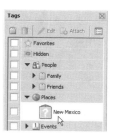

Figure 2.38 The new tag will appear in the Tags pane under the assigned category or sub-category.

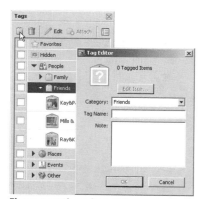

Figure 2.39 If you first click on a particular tag category or sub-category, Photoshop Album will automatically assign your tag to that category.

CREATING A NEW TAG

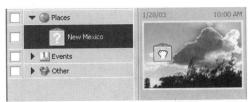

Figure 2.41 To attach tags to a single photo, click and drag any tag from the Tags pane onto a photo in the Photo Well.

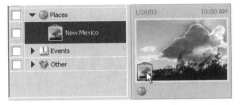

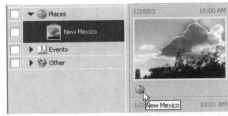

Figure 2.42 The tag's icon appears briefly after attaching it to a photo (top). Roll the cursor over the category icon to see the name of the attached tag (bottom).

To attach tags to a single photo:

◆ Click and drag any tag from the Tags pane onto a photo in the Photo Well (**Figure 2.41**). Release your cursor and the tag will be applied to the photo, with the tag icon briefly appearing atop the photo (top, **Figure 2.42**). An icon representing the tag's category will appear in the lower-left corner of the photo (bottom, **Figure 2.42**).

✔ Tips

■ If you roll your cursor over the category icon in the photo's lower-left corner, you can immediately see the name of the attached tag (bottom, **Figure 2.42**).

■ Be sure the *Show Dates* box is checked in the Options bar, otherwise the icons will not appear in the Photo Well.

■ As you can see in **Figure 2.42**, the *?* previously shown as the tag icon has been replaced by a thumbnail of the attached photo. To change the thumbnail image applied to the tag icon, see page 40.

■ Remember that you can attach multiple tags to the same photo, such as "New Mexico," "Summer Trip," and "Ray & Kerry." For more information on organizing your tags, see page 39.

To attach tags to multiple photos:

1. Within the Photo Well, [Shift]-click to select adjacent photos or [Ctrl]-click to select non-adjacent photos. Each selected photo will be surrounded by a bright yellow border.

2. Click and drag any tag from the Tags pane onto any of the selected photos (**Figure 2.43**). Release your cursor and the tag will be applied to the photos (**Figure 2.44**).

   or

   Click the Attach icon in the Tags toolbar (top, **Figure 2.45**). The tag will be applied to the photos.

   or

   From the Menu bar, choose Tag > Attach Selected Tag (bottom, **Figure 2.45**). The tag will be applied to the photos.

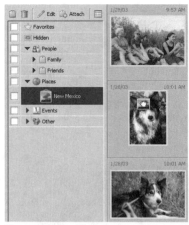

Figure 2.43 To attach tags to multiple photos, drag any tag from the Tags pane onto any of the selected photos.

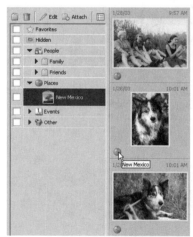

Figure 2.44 The tag after being applied to all three photos.

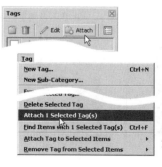

Figure 2.45 You also can attach tags to photos by clicking the Attach icon in the Tags toolbar (top) or by choosing Tag > Attach Selected Tag (bottom).

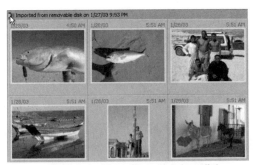

Figure 2.46 Click the film roll icon to select all the photos in that particular import batch.

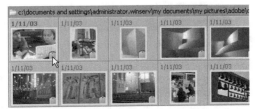

Figure 2.47 The selected tag after being attached to all the photos in a particular folder.

To attach a tag to an import batch or folder:

1. Click the Photo Well arrangement menu in the Options bar and choose Import Batch or Folder Location from the pop-up menu.

2. Scroll through the Photo Well until you find the import batch or folder to which you want to attach a tag.

3. In the Photo Well, click the film roll icon for a particular import batch or the folder icon for a folder's worth of images. All the photos in the batch or folder will be selected, with a bright yellow frame around each photo (**Figure 2.46**).

4. Click and drag any tag from the Tags pane onto any of the selected photos.

   or

   Click the Attach icon in the Tags toolbar.

   or

   From the Menu bar, choose Tag > Attach Selected Tag.

5. Release your cursor and the tag will be applied to all the photos in the import batch or folder, indicated by the small tag icon in the lower-right of each photo (**Figure 2.47**).

To remove tags from photos:

1. Within the Photo Well, select the photo with a tag you want to remove (⟨Shift⟩-click to select adjacent photos; ⟨Ctrl⟩-click to select non-adjacent photos).

2. Right-click any of the selected photos and from the drop-down menu, choose Remove Tag > [the tag you want removed] (top, **Figure 2.48**). The tag(s) will be removed (**Figure 2.49**).

   or

   From the Menu bar, choose Tag > Remove Tag > [the tag you want removed] (bottom, **Figure 2.48**). The tag(s) will be removed (**Figure 2.49**).

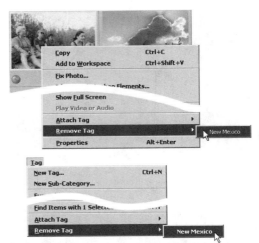

Figure 2.48 To remove tags from selected photos, right-click them and choose Remove Tag from Selected Items > [the tag you want removed] (top) or choose Tag > Remove Tag from Selected Items > [the tag you want removed] (bottom).

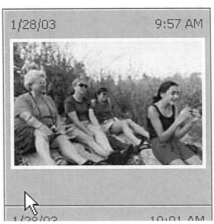

Figure 2.49 The photo's blank lower-left corner shows that all tags have been removed.

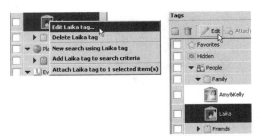

Figure 2.50 To change a tag category, name, or note, right-click on the tag you want changed (left), or click the Edit icon in the Tags toolbar (right).

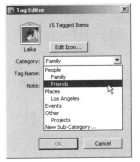

Figure 2.51 Use the *Category* drop-down menu to choose another category.

Organizing Tags

Photoshop Album has four overall category tags: People, Places, Events, and Other. You cannot create any other categories of your own, but you can create as many sub-categories as you need within each category. By default, the People category already has two useful sub-categories: Family and Friends, which can be changed to suit your needs. Remember that Photoshop Album automatically tracks your photos by date, which means that you should not be creating sub-categories under the Events category for every month and day. For more information on using the Favorites and Hidden tags, see page 45.

To change a tag category, name, or note:

1. Within the Tags pane, right-click on the tag you want changed and choose *Edit [name of] tag* from the drop-down menu (left, **Figure 2.50**).

   or

   Click the Edit icon in the Tags toolbar (right, **Figure 2.50**).

   or

   From the Menu bar, choose Tag > Edit Selected Tag.

2. When the Tag Editor dialog box appears, use the *Category* drop-down menu to choose another category (**Figure 2.51**).

3. To change the *Tag Name*, just type in a new name in the text window.

4. To change the *Note*, add or delete text in the adjacent text window.

5. Click *OK* to close the dialog box, and the changes will be applied to the tag.

ORGANIZING TAGS

To change a tag icon's appearance:

1. Within the Tags pane, right-click on the tag whose icon you want to change and from the drop-down menu choose *Edit [name of] tag* (**Figure 2.50**).

2. When the Tag Editor dialog box appears, click *Edit Icon* (**Figure 2.52**).

3. When the Tag Icon Editor dialog box appears, click *Find* (**Figure 2.53**).

4. A dialog box will display all the photos with this tag attached (**Figure 2.54**). Make your choice and click *OK* to close the dialog box.

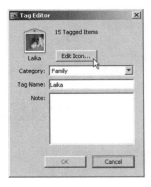

Figure 2.52
To change a tag icon's appearance, click *Edit Icon* in the Tag Icon Editor dialog box.

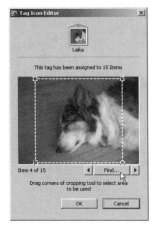

Figure 2.53
Click *Find* to look through all the photos with this tag attached.

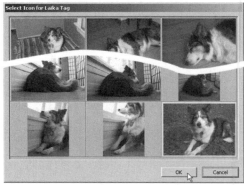

Figure 2.54 Once you choose a new photo to use, click *OK* to close the dialog box.

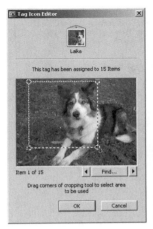

Figure 2.55
Click inside the dashed-line box to recenter the framing and grab its corner to zoom in or out on the photo.

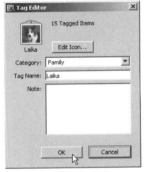

Figure 2.56
The Tag Editor dialog box reappears with the new icon choice selected. Click *OK* to close the dialog box.

5. When the Tag Icon Editor dialog box reappears, a dashed-line box will surround your new photo choice. Click inside the dashed-line box to recenter the framing and grab its corner to zoom in or out on the photo (**Figure 2.55**). When you finish, click *OK*.

6. The Tag Editor dialog box will reappear and reflect the change (**Figure 2.56**). Unless you need to make other changes, click *OK* to close the dialog box.

✔ Tip

■ At the beginning of step 3, a note above the photo tells you how many items the tag has been applied to. If the number is less than a dozen, just click the arrows on each side of the *Find* button to quickly scroll through the available icon photos.

To create a sub-category tag:

1. Within the Tags pane, right-click a tag category and choose *Create new sub-category in [Name of] category* from the drop-down menu (top, **Figure 2.57**).

   or

   From the Menu bar, choose Tag > New Sub-Category (bottom, **Figure 2.57**).

2. When the Create New Sub-Category dialog box appears, type your new sub-category in the *Sub-Category Name* text window (**Figure 2.58**).

3. The *Category* will already be listed, based on what you right-clicked in step 1. If you want to change it, use the drop-down menu.

4. Click *OK* to close the dialog box and the new sub-category will appear in the Tags pane under the originally selected category (**Figure 2.59**). You can now begin creating new tags within the sub-category (**Figure 2.60**).

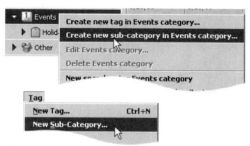

Figure 2.57 To create a sub-category tag, right-click on the category tag and choose *Create new sub-category in [Name of] category* from the drop-down menu (top), or choose Tag > New Sub-Category (bottom).

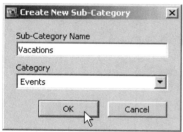

Figure 2.58 Type your new sub-category in the *Sub-Category Name* text window.

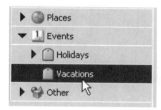

Figure 2.59 The new sub-category will appear in the Tags pane under the originally selected category.

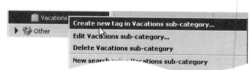

Figure 2.60 Once you create a sub-category, you can begin to create new tags for it.

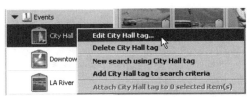

Figure 2.61 To reassign tags, right-click on the tag and choose *Edit [name of] tag* from the drop-down menu.

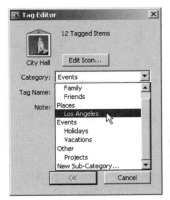

Figure 2.62 Use the *Category* drop-down menu to choose another category or sub-category.

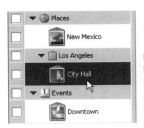

Figure 2.63 After closing the Tag Editor dialog box, the tag will appear under the newly selected category or sub-category.

To reassign tags to another category or sub-category:

1. Within the Tags pane, right-click on the tag you want to reassign and choose *Edit [name of] tag* from the drop-down menu (**Figure 2.61**).

   or

   Click the Edit icon in the Tags toolbar.

   or

   From the Menu bar, choose Tag > Edit Selected Tag.

2. When the Tag Editor dialog box appears, use the *Category* drop-down menu to choose another category or sub-category (**Figure 2.62**).

3. Click *OK* to close the dialog box and the tag will appear under the selected category or sub-category within the Tags pane (**Figure 2.63**).

To expand or collapse the tags view:

◆ From the Menu bar, choose Tag > Expand All or Tag > Collapse All (**Figure 2.64**). Depending on your choice, all the categories and sub-categories will appear in the Tags pane or only the six categories will appear (**Figure 2.65**).

✔ Tip

■ To expand or collapse only selected categories or sub-categories, click the left-side triangles in the Tags pane (**Figure 2.66**).

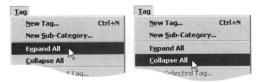

Figure 2.64 To expand or collapse tags in the Tags pane, choose Tag > Expand All or Tag > Collapse All.

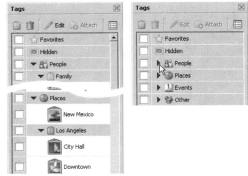

Figure 2.65 The Tags pane with all tag categories expanded (left) and collapsed (right).

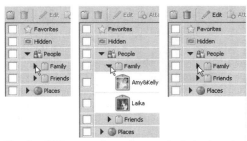

Figure 2.66 To expand or collapse selected categories or sub-categories, click the left-side triangles in the Tags pane.

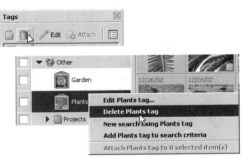

Figure 2.67 To delete a selected tag, click the Trash icon in the Tags toolbar (top) or right-click the tag and choose *Delete [Name of] tag* from the drop-down menu (bottom).

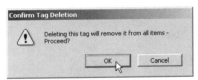

Figure 2.68 Once you click *OK* in the Confirm Tag Deletion dialog box, the tag will be deleted.

To delete a tag:

1. Click the tag you want to delete and then click the Trash icon in the Tags toolbar (top, **Figure 2.67**).

   or

   Within the Tags pane, right-click the tag you want to delete and choose *Delete [Name of] tag* from the drop-down menu (bottom, **Figure 2.67**).

2. When the Confirm Tag Deletion dialog box appears, click *OK* (**Figure 2.68**). The tag will be deleted from the Tags pane.

✔ Tips

- If you mistakenly delete the wrong tag (it's bound to happen), choose Edit > Undo Delete Tag(s) (Ctrl Z).

- If you have a bunch of tags to delete, you can Shift-click to select adjacent tags; Ctrl-click to select non-adjacent tags.

Using the Favorites and Hidden Tags

While technically category tags, Favorites and Hidden are most useful when combined with *sub-category* tags. Use the Favorites tag to mark your best shots within a particular sub-category. While you can search only for photos marked Favorites, the tag becomes more useful and powerful when you combine it with other tags already applied to your photos. That way, you can quickly see your favorite shots within a particular category or sub-category. Similarly use the Hidden tag with other category and sub-category tags. If you have a project with hundreds of photos, which you don't want cluttering up the Photo Well, for example, attach the Hidden tag and they'll be tucked out of sight. Photos tagged as Hidden will not appear even when you click the Show All icon. The only way Hidden photos appear is if you select the checkbox next to the Hidden tag in the Tags pane. You can quickly gauge how many photos have been marked hidden using the Timeline (see page 59).

Working with Catalogs

Photoshop Album stores your tags, captions, notes, and categories in a catalog—without ever actually changing the original photos themselves. In most cases, you don't even need to think about the catalog, which is really a multimedia database. Just remember one thing about catalogs: Back them up right now, back them up regularly, and you'll be safe should anything ever go wrong.

While making a backup, you'll need to stay at the computer but you won't be able to use Photoshop Album. If you're backing up to a CD or DVD (also known as archiving), the whole process can take up to 20 minutes. While that seems slow, it could spare you hours of frustration later on. So go get yourself some coffee or the newspaper, and come back to your desk to start the backup.

Should anything ever go wrong with your catalogs, Photoshop Album offers two options: recover and restore. If your computer crashes while you are working in Photoshop Album, the recover catalog process will attempt to repair any damage. If the recovery fails, you can try to restore the catalog from your backup catalog, although any changes made since your last backup will not be restored, so use it only as a last resort. You also can use the restore process to retrieve photos from the backup that you accidentally deleted from your current catalog.

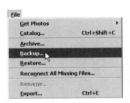

Figure 2.69 To backup or archive your catalog, chose File > Backup.

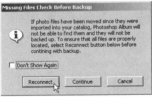

Figure 2.70 Click *Reconnect* to make sure none of the Photoshop Album files have been moved from their original locations.

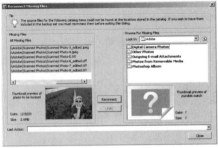

Figure 2.71 Photoshop Album will list *Missing Files* that have been moved in the left-hand pane, above a thumbnail of the first missing file.

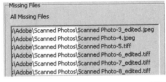

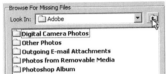

Figure 2.72 In this example, all the missing files had been in the same folder: *Scanned Photos* (top). Use the *Browse For Missing Files* pane icons to navigate to the missing folder.

To backup your catalog:

1. From the Menu bar, chose File > Backup (**Figure 2.69**).

2. When the Missing Files Check Before Backup dialog box appears, click *Reconnect* to make sure that none of the Photoshop Album files have been moved from their original locations (**Figure 2.70**).

3. If no files have been moved, the left-hand *Missing Files* pane in the Reconnect Missing Files dialog box will be blank, and you can click *Close* and skip to step 6.

   or

   If Photoshop Album cannot find some files because they have been moved, a list will appear in the left-hand *Missing Files* pane of the Reconnect Missing Files dialog box, just above a thumbnail of the first missing file (**Figure 2.71**).

4. In most cases, the missing files originally will have been in the same folder (in this case, \Adobe\Scanned Photos\), so Ctrl-click to select all the files with the same folder in common, then use the right-hand *Browse For Missing Files* pane icons to navigate to that missing folder (**Figure 2.72**). (Use the Start menu to choose Search > For Files or Folders if you don't know where a folder's been moved.)

(continued on next page)

5. Once you select the correct missing folder, both thumbnails in the dialog box will match, and you can click *Reconnect* (**Figure 2.73**). Once the files have been reconnected, the left-hand Missing Files pane will be blank and you can click *Close*.

6. When the Backup dialog box appears, if you choose a drive as your backup target (left, **Figure 2.74**), you'll need to navigate to the chosen drive and folder. Or select *Burn onto a CD or DVD Disc* and your disc burner will be automatically selected (right, **Figure 2.74**). You also have the choice of making a *Full Backup* or an *Incremental Backup* (see the *Tip* on the next page). Once you've made your choices, click *OK* to close the dialog box.

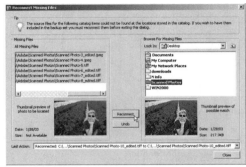

Figure 2.73 Once you select the correct missing folder, the thumbnails in the dialog box will match, and you can click *Reconnect*.

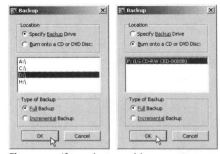

Figure 2.74 If you choose a drive as your backup target, you'll need to navigate to the chosen drive and folder (left). If you select *Burn onto a CD or DVD Disc*, your disc burner will be automatically selected (right).

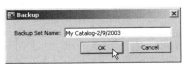

Figure 2.75 When the Backup dialog box appears, name the backup and click *OK*.

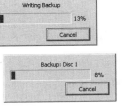

Figure 2.76
A status bar will track the backup process to your hard drive (top) or disc burner (bottom).

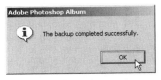

Figure 2.77 If you backed up to a hard drive, you're done (top). If you backed up to a disc, you still need to verify that the disc burned correctly (bottom).

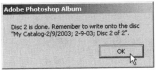

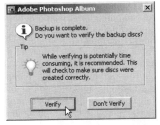

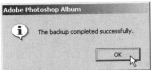

Figure 2.78 Click *Verify* and follow the dialog box prompts to test the disc(s) (top). Once the testing is done, click *OK* to close the dialog box (bottom).

7. When the Backup dialog box appears, name the backup and click *OK* (**Figure 2.75**). A status bar will track the backup process (**Figure 2.76**) until it's complete (**Figure 2.77**). Click *OK* to close the dialog box and if you backed up to a hard drive, you're done.

8. If you backed up to a disc, there's one last crucial step: verifying that the disc was burned correctly (top, **Figure 2.78**). Click *Verify* and follow the dialog box prompts to test the disc(s). Once the testing is complete, click *OK* to close the dialog box (bottom, **Figure 2.78**). Now you really are done—except for marking your calendar for your next backup.

✔ Tip

■ If this is your first time backing up the Photoshop Album catalog, in step 6 choose *Full Backup*. If you've only added a few photos to the catalog since your last backup, you can choose Incremental Backup, which will not take as long as a full backup. In most cases, it's best to burn a backup to a disc instead of backing up to your hard drive. That way, if your computer fails entirely, you'll still have a copy of the catalog. Make a second set of backup discs to keep at the office in case disaster hits your home.

To recover a catalog

1. From the Menu bar, chose File > Catalog ([Ctrl] [Shift] [C]) (**Figure 2.79**).

2. When the Catalog dialog box appears, click *Recover* (**Figure 2.80**).

3. When the Recover Catalog dialog box appears, click *OK* (**Figure 2.81**). A status bar will appear briefly and then—if all goes well—a dialog box will announce that the recovery was successful (**Figure 2.82**). Click *OK* to close the dialog box and begin working with the recovered catalog. If the recovery fails, see *To restore a catalog* on the next page.

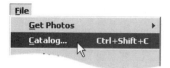

Figure 2.79 To recover a damaged catalog, create a new catalog, or switch catalogs, start by choosing File > Catalog.

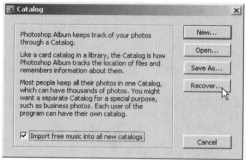

Figure 2.80 When the Catalog dialog box appears, click *Recover*.

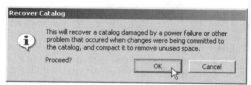

Figure 2.81 When the Recover Catalog dialog box appears, click *OK*.

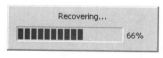

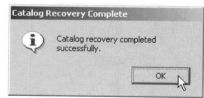

Figure 2.82 A status bar will appear briefly (top) and, if all goes well, a dialog box will announce that the recovery was successful (bottom).

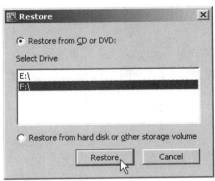

Figure 2.83 When restoring a catalog, the CD/DVD option is selected by default. If the backup is on a hard drive, select *Restore from hard disk or other storage volume* instead.

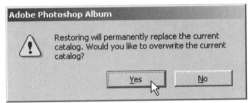

Figure 2.84 If you could not recover the original catalog, click *Yes* to begin the restore process.

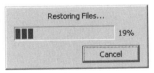

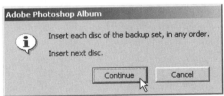

Figure 2.85 A status bar will track the restoration from the first disc (top). If the backup resides on more than one disc, you'll be asked to insert each disc in turn (bottom).

To restore a catalog

1. If your backup catalog is on a CD or DVD, insert it into your disc drive. If your backup is on another hard drive, make sure it's connected to your computer.

2. From the Menu bar, chose File > Restore.

3. When the Restore dialog box appears, the CD/DVD option is selected by default (**Figure 2.83**). Use the *Select Drive* window to choose a disc drive or, if the backup is on a hard drive, select *Restore from hard disk or other storage volume*. Once you make your selection, click *Restore*.

4. A dialog box will appear asking you to insert any disc from the backup set, if you haven't already done so. Click *Continue* and another dialog box will warn you that this will overwrite your current catalog. If you could not recover the original catalog, click *Yes* to begin the restore process (**Figure 2.84**).

5. Depending on the status of your current catalog, you may see yet another dialog box warning that you are about to overwrite files that already exist. Once again, if you could not recover the catalog, click *Yes to All*. A status bar will appear, tracking the restoration from the first disc (top, **Figure 2.85**).

(continued on next page)

RESTORING A CATALOG

6. If the backup resides on more than one disc, a dialog box will ask you to insert another disk (bottom, **Figure 2.85**). Click *Continue*, and another status bar will appear, and the dialog box prompts will continue to appear until all the backup discs have been inserted.

7. Once the restoration is completed, the Photo Well will be redrawn. Some items, particularly videos or photo projects (called creations in Photoshop Album), may take a bit longer to reappear. While they are being restored, their place will be marked by an hourglass icon and an hourglass will rotate at the bottom-right corner of the Photo Well (**Figure 2.86**).

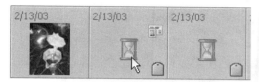

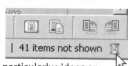

Figure 2.86 Some items, particularly videos or projects, may take a bit longer to restore. In the meantime, their place will be marked by an hourglass icon (top) and an hourglass will rotate at the bottom of the Photo Well (bottom).

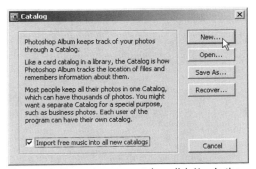

Figure 2.87 To create a new catalog, click *New* in the Catalog dialog box.

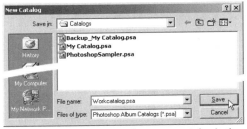

Figure 2.88 Type the name of your new catalog in the *File name* text window and click *Save*.

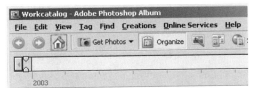

Figure 2.89 The timeline for the new, empty catalog will show no imports. You can begin importing photos and building new tags for the catalog.

Making, Switching, or Copying Catalogs

The only limit on the size of a catalog is the capacity of your hard drive. So in most cases, you'll never need to create another catalog in Photoshop Album. That's especially true since the sub-category tags can accomplish many of the same things without the potential confusion of having multiple catalogs. If, however, you have more than one person using Photoshop Album on the same computer or you need a business-only catalog as well, it may be useful to create several catalogs. There are several drawbacks, however. You can only work with one catalog at a time, and photos and tags cannot be moved from one catalog to another.

A copy of a catalog does not copy any of the images stored in the original catalog. It only copies the original's tags and tag organization. However, that can be useful if you or someone else wants to create a new catalog using the tags you've already created.

To create a new catalog:

1. From the Menu bar, chose File > Catalog ([Ctrl][Shift][C]) (**Figure 2.79**).

2. When the Catalog dialog box appears, click *New* (**Figure 2.87**).

3. When the New Catalog dialog box appears, it will include a list of your existing catalogs. Type the name of your new catalog in the *File name* text window and click *Save* (**Figure 2.88**). Photoshop Album will close your previous catalog and display the new, empty catalog, whose timeline will show no imports (**Figure 2.89**). You can now begin importing new photos and building new tags for the catalog.

To switch catalogs:

1. From the Menu bar, chose File > Catalog (⌃Ctrl ⇧Shift C) (**Figure 2.79**).

2. When the Catalog dialog box appears, click *Open* (**Figure 2.90**).

3. When the New Catalog or Open Catalog dialog box appears, it will list all your catalogs. Select a catalog, such as your original catalog, and click *Open* (**Figure 2.91**). Your current catalog will close and the selected catalog will open.

To copy a catalog:

1. From the Menu bar, chose File > Catalog (⌃Ctrl ⇧Shift C) (**Figure 2.79**).

2. When the Catalog dialog box appears, click *Save As* and navigate to where you want to store the copy.

3. Type a name for the copy in the *File name* text box and click *Save*. The copy will be created and saved.

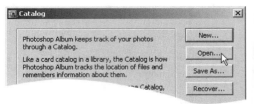

Figure 2.90 To switch catalogs, click *Open* in the Catalog dialog box.

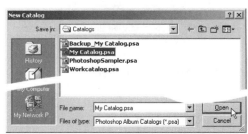

Figure 2.91 To use another catalog, select it in the Open Catalog dialog box and click *Open*.

3

FINDING PHOTOS

When you import photos into Photoshop Album, the program automatically notes their creation date, import batch, and original location. The program also keeps track of whether the photos came from your digital camera, a scanner, or a folder on your computer. With that detailed information stored within Photoshop Album, you have dozens of ways to track down a particular photo. The timeline and calendar view provide two powerful tools for finding photos by date. And remember, your ability to find your photos also includes the tags you used to organize your photos in Chapter 2.

Finding Photos by Tags

Just as Photoshop Album gives you the flexibility to organize your photos with customized tags, it lets you harness the power of those tags to find individual photos or groups of photos. As always, you have several ways to use tags in such searches.

Ways to find photos by tag:

◆ Make sure the Tags pane is visible (**Ctrl** **T**), then double-click any tag in the pane. Photos with that tag will appear in the Photo Well (**Figure 3.1**).

◆ Select the blank box to the left of the tag. Photos with that tag will appear in the Photo Well (**Figure 3.1**).

◆ Click-and-drag a tag into the Find bar (the light blue strip just above the Photo Well) (**Figure 3.2**). Photos with that tag will appear in the Photo Well (**Figure 3.1**).

◆ From the Menu bar, choose Find > Items Tagged With and then navigate to the particular tag you want to use (**Figure 3.3**). Photos with that tag will appear in the Photo Well (**Figure 3.1**).

✔ Tips

■ Within the Tags pane, a binoculars icon will appear next to the tag used for the search. The tag also will appear in the Find bar, along with a note on how many items matched that tag and how many items did not (**Figure 3.1**).

■ You can also search for photos that have no tags attached by choosing Find > Untagged Items.

■ To see photos that do not match the chosen tag(s), check *Not Matching* and uncheck *Matching* in the Find bar (**Figure 3.1**).

■ To find photos tagged Hidden, double-click the Hidden tag in the Tags pane.

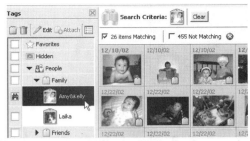

Figure 3.1 Double-click any tag in the Tags pane, and photos with that tag will appear in the Photo Well.

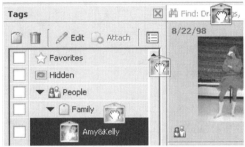

Figure 3.2 To find tagged photos, you also can click-and-drag a tag into the Find bar.

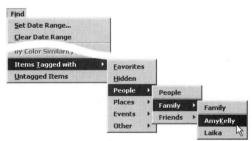

Figure 3.3 A third way to find tagged photos: choose Find > Items Tagged With and then navigate to the particular tag you want used.

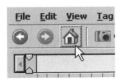

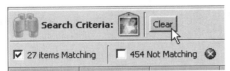

Figure 3.4 To cancel a find, click the Show All icon in the Shortcuts bar (top) or click the *Clear* button in the Find bar (bottom).

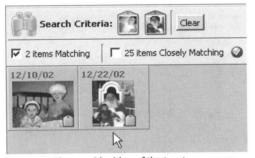

Figure 3.5 Photos with either of the two tags appearing in the Find bar will appear in the Photo Well.

Ways to cancel a find:

◆ Click the Show All icon in the Shortcuts bar (top, **Figure 3.4**). All your photos will reappear in the Photo Well.

◆ Click the *Clear* button in the Find bar (the light blue strip at the top of the Photo Well) (bottom, **Figure 3.4**). All your photos will reappear in the Photo Well.

◆ Press the Spacebar and all your photos will reappear in the Photo Well.

Ways to find photos using multiple tags:

◆ Make sure the Tags pane is visible (Ctrl T), then select the blank box to the left of each tag you want included in the search. Photos tagged with any *one* of those tags will appear in the Photo Well (**Figure 3.5**). The Photo Well will update automatically as you select more tags.

◆ Click-and-drag each tag into the Find bar that you want used in the search. As you drag additional tags into the Find bar, photos with those tags will appear in the Photo Well (**Figure 3.5**). The Photo Well will update automatically as you drag more tags to the Find bar. See *Understanding Multiple-Tag Searches* on page 58 for more information on how Photoshop Album handles multiple-tag searches.

✔ Tip

■ As you search for photos, selecting and then unselecting tags, you may start finding photos you don't remember seeking. One explanation: A tag hidden from view in the Tags pane remains accidentally selected. From the Menu bar, choose Tag > Expand All to see if that's the case.

Understanding Multiple-Tag Searches

When making a multiple-tag search, the results will vary depending on whether any of the photos have more than one tag attached. Taking a look at the Find bar shows how this works in some example searches:

◆ In **Figure 3.6,** the Find bar shows *1 item Matching* all three of the selected tags (*Jim&Lenora, Kay&Paul*, and *Ray&Kerry*). The Find bar also shows *67 items Closely Matching,* which means that 67 photos have at least one of the three tags attached.

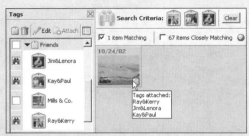

Figure 3.6 Only one photo matches exactly by having all three tags. Another 67 items closely match by having at least one of the three tags.

◆ In **Figure 3.7,** the other 67 photos appear after selecting *67 items Closely Matching* in the Find bar. Rolling the cursor over one of those 67 photos in the Photo Well confirms why it's just a close and not exact match: It only has the *Jim&Lenora* tag attached.

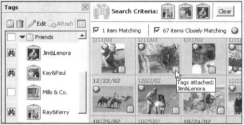

Figure 3.7 Checking *67 Items Closely Matching* shows the other photos tagged with at least one of the three tags.

◆ After removing all but one of the three tags originally attached to the photo in **Figure 3.6** (leaving it tagged only with *Ray&Kerry*), a new search now shows that no photos match all three selected tags. Instead, the Find bar shows *68 items Closely Matching* (**Figure 3.8**).

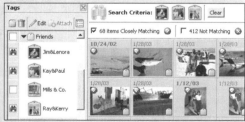

Figure 3.8 After removing all but one of the three tags originally attached to the photo in Figure 3.6, a new search shows no photos that match all three selected tags. Instead, the Find bar shows *68 items Closely Matching.*

Finding Photos by Date

At first, the timeline might seem almost dull. But once you learn how to combine it with the Photo Well's sorting ability, you'll find it one of the most effective ways to find photos. While also using dates, the calendar view offers a more graphical way to help you find those photos immediately. It's also great for special events with set dates, such as birthdays and holidays. Photoshop Album even includes a way to find undated photos.

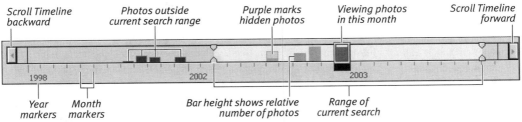

Figure 3.9 The timeline contains enough information to create precise photo searches.

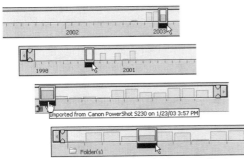

Figure 3.10 The timeline display changes to reflect how you've sorted the Photo Well: newest first (top), oldest first (2nd from top), import batch (2nd from bottom), or folder (bottom).

To find photos with the timeline:

1. If the timeline is not visible, from the Menu bar choose View > Timeline and the timeline will appear (**Figure 3.9**).

2. To choose how you want the photos sorted, click the Photo Well arrangement pop-up menu in the Options bar (or Ctrl Alt 0 to see the newest photos first, Ctrl Alt 1 to arrange with the oldest first, Ctrl Alt 2 to see by import batch, or Ctrl Alt 3 to see based on folder location). The timeline will change to reflect your choice (**Figure 3.10**).

(continued on next page)

FINDING PHOTOS BY DATE

3. Click and drag the timeline's endpoints to adjust the date range you want to search (**Figure 3.11**). The Photo Well will display the results.

or

From the Menu bar, choose Find > Set Date Range and when the Set Date Range dialog box appears, use the text windows and drop-down menus to define the range you want searched (**Figure 3.12**). Click *OK* and the Photo Well will display the results (**Figures 3.13–3.15**).

✔ Tip

■ Unless you have an exact date you are searching for, clicking and dragging the timeline's endpoints is faster than using the Set Date Range dialog box.

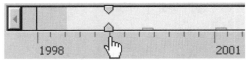

Figure 3.11 Click and drag the timeline's endpoints to adjust the date range you want to search.

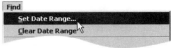

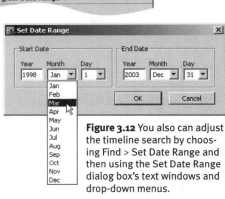

Figure 3.12 You also can adjust the timeline search by choosing Find > Set Date Range and then using the Set Date Range dialog box's text windows and drop-down menus.

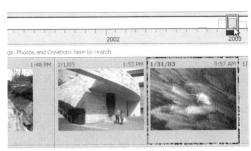

Figure 3.13 With Photo Well sorting set to newest first, the search results will mark with a green border the newest photo of that month (in this case, a photo dated 1/31).

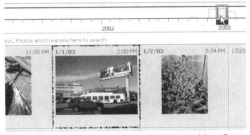

Figure 3.14 With Photo Well sorting set to oldest first, the search results will mark with a green border the oldest photo of that month (in this case, a photo dated 1/1).

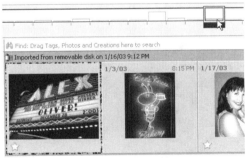

Figure 3.15 With Photo Well sorting set to import batch, the search results will mark with a green border the first photo imported in that batch.

To find tagged photos with the timeline:

1. Click and drag a tag or tags from the Tags pane into the Find bar—just as you did in using Tags to find photos. The Photo Well will display only photos with that tag or tags.

2. Now click and drag the timeline's end-points to adjust the date range for where you want to find specific tagged photos. The results in the Photo Well will update to show the search results.

To find photos with the calendar view:

1. In the Shortcuts bar, click the *Calendar* icon (top, **Figure 3.16**) and the calendar view window will appear (**Figure 3.17**).

   or

   In the Menu bar, choose View > Calendar ([Ctrl][Alt][C]) (bottom, **Figure 3.16**) and the calendar view window will appear (**Figure 3.17**).

2. To see another month, click the back and forward arrows at the top of the month (beneath the photo currently displayed), or click the name of the month and make a choice from the drop-down menu (**Figure 3.18**).

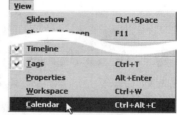

Figure 3.16 To find photos with the calendar view, click the *Calendar* icon (top), or choose View > Calendar (bottom).

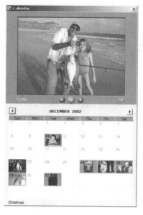

Figure 3.17 The calendar view displays the selected photo in the top window and in the bottom grid shows every day when photos were imported.

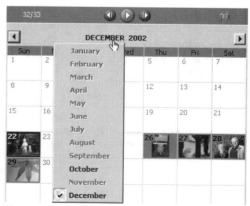

Figure 3.18 To see another month in the calendar view, click the arrows at the top of the month, or click the name of the month and make a choice from the drop-down menu.

Place in day's photos | *See day's previous photo* | *See day's next photo* | *See selection in Photo Well*

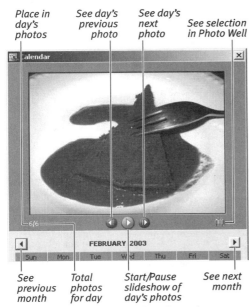

See previous month | *Total photos for day* | *Start/Pause slideshow of day's photos* | *See next month*

Figure 3.19 Once you find the day whose photos you want to view, use the window's back and forward buttons to scroll through the day's photos or click the center button to see them all in sequence.

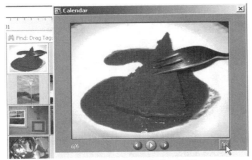

Figure 3.20 Click the calendar window's binoculars icon (far right) and the photo will be highlighted in the Photo Well with a bright yellow border (left).

3. Once you reach the desired month, click the day in the grid whose photos you want to view and the first photo of that day will appear in the top of the calendar window (**Figure 3.19**). Use the window's back and forward buttons to scroll through the day's photos or click the center button to see them all in sequence.

4. Once you find the desired photo, click the calendar window's binoculars icon and the photo will be highlighted in the Photo Well with a bright yellow border (**Figure 3.20**).

✔ Tips

■ In step 2, months without any photos will be grayed out in the drop-down menu.

■ To jump to another year, use the drop-down menu to choose January or December, then click the back or forward arrow to move to the preceding or next year.

■ When the calendar view first appears, reposition the window so you also can see the Photo Well and the window will open in that spot every time afterward.

To find photos by unknown dates:

◆ From the Menu bar, choose Find > Items with Unknown Date or Time. The Photo Well will display all photos with no set date or time.

✔ Tip

■ If you want to add a date or time to any of the photos, see *To change a photo's date or time* on page 31.

FINDING PHOTOS WITH CALENDAR VIEW

Other Ways to Find Photos

Given the powers of catalogs within Photoshop Album, it's no surprise that Photoshop Album includes dozens of other ways to find photos (**Figure 3.21**).

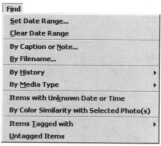

Figure 3.21 The extensive Find menu includes just about every imaginable way to find a photo.

To find photos by filename:

1. From the Menu bar, choose Find > By Filename.

2. When the Find by Filename dialog box appears, type in part or all of the name and click *OK* (**Figure 3.22**). Photos with filenames containing the text will appear in the Photo Well.

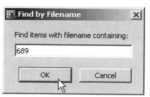

Figure 3.22 When the Find by Filename dialog box appears, type in part or all of the name and click *OK*.

To find photos by caption or note:

1. From the Menu bar, choose Find > By Caption or Note (**Figure 3.23**).

2. When the Find by Caption or Note dialog box appears, type in part or all of the caption or note for the photo you are seeking (**Figure 3.24**). Use the two radio buttons below the text window to fine-tune your search and click *OK*. The Find bar will tell you how many photo captions or notes contain the text, and the first matching photo will appear in the Photo Well (**Figure 3.25**).

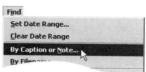

Figure 3.23 To find photos by caption or note, choose Find > By Caption or Note.

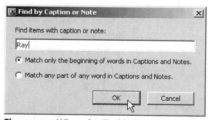

Figure 3.24 When the Find by Caption or Note dialog box appears, type in part or all of the caption or note for the photo you are seeking.

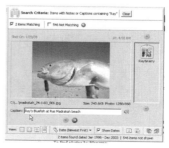

Figure 3.25 The Find bar will list how many photo captions or notes contain matching text, and the first matching photo will appear in the Photo Well.

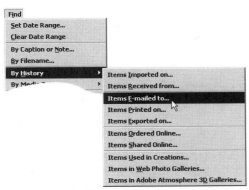

Figure 3.26 To find photos by history, choose Find > By History and then make a choice from the drop-down menu.

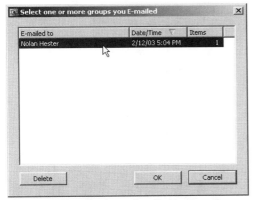

Figure 3.27 Choosing *Items E-mailed to* prompts Photoshop Album to show a list of recipients of emailed photos.

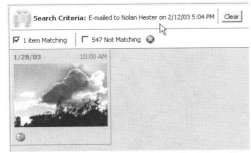

Figure 3.28 All photos mailed to the selected email recipient will appear in the Photo Well.

To find photos by history:

1. From the Menu bar, choose Find > By History and then make a choice from the drop-down menu (**Figure 3.26**).

2. In this example, choosing *Items E-mailed to* prompts Photoshop Album to show a list of recipients of emailed photos (**Figure 3.27**).

3. Make a selection in the dialog box and click *OK*. The results will appear in the Photo Well and the Find bar will display details of the search (**Figure 3.28**).

✔ Tip

■ As you can see in the drop-down menu in **Figure 3.26**, Photoshop Album automatically tracks virtually everything you might do with a photo: import or export it, print or share it, use it in a Photoshop Album project (called a creation) or on the Web, to name just a few of the choices.

To find photos by media type:

◆ From the Menu bar, choose Find > By Media Type and then make a choice from the drop-down menu (**Figure 3.29**). The Photo Well will display all the items matching your drop-down menu choice.

To find photos of similar color:

1. In the Photo Well, select a photo or photos where the predominant colors come close to the colors you want to find in other photos (such as the orange of autumn leaves).

2. Drag the selected photo(s) into the Find bar, or choose Find > By Color Similarity with Selected Photo(s) (**Figure 3.30**). Photos with similar colors to the selected photos will appear in the Photo Well (**Figure 3.31**).

✔ Tips

■ The initial search results in the Photo Well may include only very close color matches. To see a broader range of photos with colors similar to your original selection(s), select the Find bar's Closely Matching box (**Figure 3.32**).

■ The similar-color search can be particularly useful for finding duplicate images since the colors will be virtually the same. The Closely Matching option also can be a great tool for slideshow sequencing where you may want to break up the chronological order with clusters of, say, yellow flowers or autumn leaves.

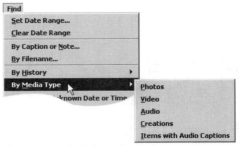

Figure 3.29 To find photos by media type, choose Find > By Media Type and then make a choice from the drop-down menu.

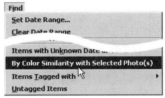

Figure 3.30 To find photos similar in color to those selected in the Photo Well, first choose Find > By Color Similarity with Selected Photo(s).

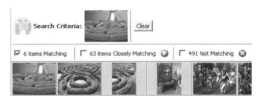

Figure 3.31 Photos with colors similar to the selected photos will then appear in the Photo Well.

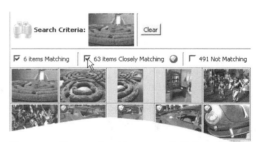

Figure 3.32 To see a broader range of photos with colors similar to your original selection(s), select the Find bar's *Closely Matching* box.

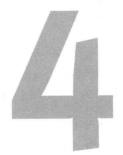

EDITING PHOTOS

Today's digital cameras are very good at nailing the correct exposure for a photo. Many also include automatic red eye reduction features, further boosting your chances of getting a perfect shot. But when you inevitably need to make some fixes to a photo—or simply want to crop it a bit tighter—Photoshop Album includes a number of easy to use photo editing controls.

To safeguard your original photo, Photoshop Album makes all your editing changes to a copy of that photo (named *originalname_edited*) and saves it in the same folder as the original. From that point on, Photoshop Album automatically opens the edited version whenever you select the original photo in the Photo Well. If you are not happy with the results of any edits, you can always revert back to the original photo.

To select photos to fix:

◆ In the Photo Well, click the photo you want to edit. (⟨Shift⟩-click to select adjacent photos or ⟨Ctrl⟩-click to select non-adjacent photos.)

To rotate photos:

1. In the Photo Well, select the photo(s) you want to rotate.

2. Click the Rotate Left or Rotate Right icon in the Options bar (**Figure 4.1**). After the Rotating Photos dialog box briefly appears, the Photo Well display will change to reflect the rotation (**Figure 4.2**).

   or

   Right-click any of the selected photos, and choose Rotate Right (⟨Ctrl⟩⟨R⟩) or Rotate Left (⟨Ctrl⟩⟨Shift⟩⟨R⟩) from the pop-up menu (**Figure 4.3**).

   or

   From the Menu bar, choose Edit > Rotate Right (⟨Ctrl⟩⟨R⟩) or Rotate Left (⟨Ctrl⟩⟨Shift⟩⟨R⟩).

✔ Tip

■ It's common to rotate your photos within the Photo Well since it lets you quickly see which ones need reorienting in a new import batch. However, you can also rotate a single photo by choosing Edit > Fix Photo and then clicking the Rotate Left or Rotate Right icons within the Fix Photo dialog box. That may be more convenient if you are making all your corrections to a single photo at the same time.

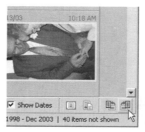

Figure 4.1 To rotate a selected photo, click the Rotate Left or Rotate Right icon in the Options bar.

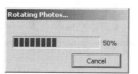

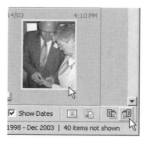

Figure 4.2 The Rotating Photos dialog box will appear briefly (top) before the Photo Well displays the rotated photo (bottom).

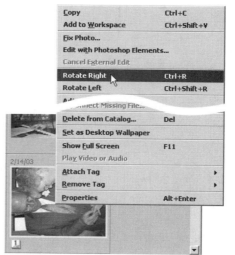

Figure 4.3 You also can right-click any selected photo and choose Rotate Right or Rotate Left from the pop-up menu.

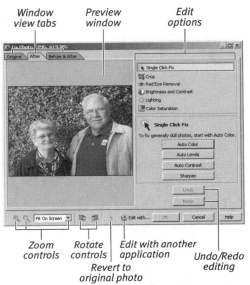

Window view tabs   Preview window   Edit options

Zoom controls   Rotate controls   Edit with another application   Undo/Redo editing

Revert to original photo

Figure 4.4 Most of your photo editing will occur using the Fix Photo dialog box.

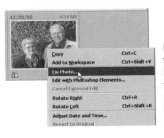

Figure 4.5 To open the Fix Photo dialog box, right-click the photo and choose Fix Photo from the pop-up menu (bottom).

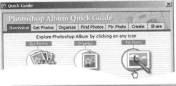

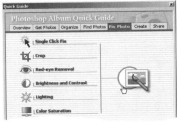

Figure 4.6 In the Quick Guide, click the *Fix Photo* icon or tab (top) and then any of six editing icons (bottom).

Using the Fix Photo Dialog Box

With the exception of rotating photos within the Photo Well, you'll do virtually all your photo editing using the Fix Photo dialog box (**Figure 4.4**).

To open the Fix Photo dialog box:

1. In the Photo Well, select a single photo to edit.

2. Click the Fix Photo icon in the Shortcuts bar (top, **Figure 4.5**).

   or

   Right-click the photo and choose Fix Photo from the pop-up menu (bottom, **Figure 4.5**).

   or

   Use the Menu bar to choose Edit > Fix Photo.

   or

   Double-click a photo in the Photo Well and when it appears in the single view, double-click it again.

   or

   If you are using the Quick Guide, click the Fix Photo icon or tab and when the Fix Photo panel appears, click any of its six icons (**Figure 4.6**).

3. When the Fix Photo alert box appears, click *OK* (**Figure 4.7**). The selected photo will appear in the Fix Photo dialog box (**Figure 4.4**).

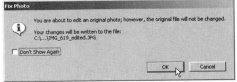

Figure 4.7 When the Fix Photo alert box appears, click *OK*.

To zoom in or out while fixing photos:

◆ In the Fix Photo dialog box, click the + or – magnifying glass icons in the bottom toolbar or use the *Fit On Screen* drop-down menu (**Figure 4.8**).

To compare before and after photo fixes:

◆ In the Fix Photo dialog box, click the *Original* tab to see the photo before any fixes (the *After* tab is selected by default). Or click the *Before & After* tab to compare the effects of your fixes as you make them (**Figure 4.9**).

✔ Tip

■ Unfortunately Photoshop Album does not let you zoom in on a photo using the *Before & After* tab, which would be really useful when you want to gauge the effects of subtle changes. The best you can do is to zoom in using the *After* tab and then click back and forth to compare it to the zoomed-in *Original* or *Before* tab.

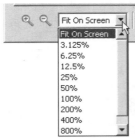

Figure 4.8 To zoom in or out while fixing photos, click the + or – icons or use the *Fit On Screen* menu.

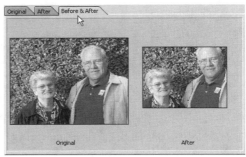

Figure 4.9 To compare before and after photo fixes, click the *Before & After* tab.

Ways to undo or redo photo fixes:

◆ If you make a fix to a photo and are not happy with the results, click *Undo* in the bottom-right of the Fix Photo dialog box.

◆ If you undo a fix and then decide you want to make the fix after all, click *Redo* in the bottom-right of the Fix Photo dialog box.

◆ If you want to cancel all your fixes and close the Fix Photo dialog box, click *Cancel* in the bottom-right of the Fix Photo dialog box.

To revert to the original photo:

◆ If you have made a series of fixes to a photo and want to return to how the photo first looked when you imported it into Photoshop Album, click the Revert button at the bottom of the Fix Photo dialog box (**Figure 4.4**). The fixes will be lost and cannot be recovered.

✔ Tip

■ You can see what the original photo looked like without clicking the Revert button by clicking the *Original* tab in the Fix Photo dialog box (**Figure 4.4**).

To crop a photo:

1. Select the photo, open the Fix Photo dialog box, and click *Crop* near the upper-right of the dialog box. A dashed rectangle will appear within your photo, indicating how the crop marks will be applied (**Figure 4.10**).

2. Use the *Select Aspect Ratio* drop-down menu in the lower-right Crop panel to choose what width-to-height proportions you want to use in applying the crop. The crop marks will change to reflect those proportions.

3. Click and drag inside the dashed rectangle to reposition the crop marks, or click and drag a corner of the dashed rectangle to shrink or expand the area to be cropped (**Figure 4.11**).

4. Once you've adjusted the crop marks to your satisfaction, click *Apply Crop* in the Crop panel. The results of the crop will appear in the left side of the Fix Photo dialog box (**Figure 4.12**). If you plan to make other fixes to the photo, leave the dialog box open. If the crop is the only fix you want to make, click *OK* and when the Fix Photo alert dialog box appears, click *OK* again to save the change (**Figure 4.13**).

✔ Tip

- In step 2, the *Select Aspect Ratio* drop-down menu only controls the width-to-height proportions of the crop, while the overall size is controlled by your adjustments in step 3.

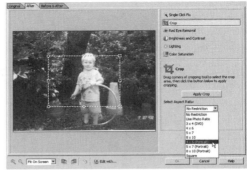

Figure 4.10 To crop a photo, click *Crop* near the upper-right of the dialog box and use the *Select Aspect Ratio* drop-down menu to choose your crop proportions.

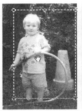 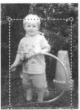 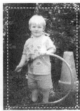

Figure 4.11 The initial crop marks (left) can be repositioned (middle) and resized (right).

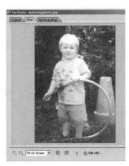

Figure 4.12 The results of your crop will appear in the Fix Photo dialog box.

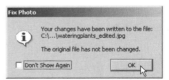

Figure 4.13 When the Fix Photo alert dialog box appears, click *OK* to save any editing changes.

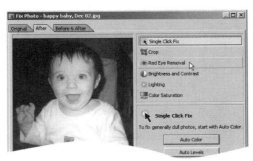

Figure 4.14 To remove red eye, click *Red Eye Removal* in the upper-right of the Fix Photo dialog box.

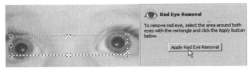

Figure 4.15 Once you've adjusted the effect's boundaries to your satisfaction, click Apply *Red Eye Removal*.

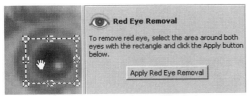

Figure 4.16 You may want to zoom in to isolate one eye at a time before clicking *Apply Red Eye Removal*.

To remove red eye:

1. Select the photo with red eye, open the Fix Photo dialog box, and click *Red Eye Removal* in the upper-right of the dialog box (**Figure 4.14**). A dashed rectangle will appear within your photo, indicating where red will be removed.

2. Click and drag inside the dashed rectangle to reposition its boundaries, or click and drag a corner or side of it to shrink or expand the area affected by red eye removal (see the first *Tip* below).

3. Once you've adjusted the boundaries to your satisfaction, click Apply *Red Eye Removal* in the Red Eye Removal panel (**Figure 4.15**). The results will appear in the left side of the Fix Photo dialog box. If you plan to make other fixes to the photo, leave the dialog box open, otherwise click *OK* and when the Fix Photo alert dialog box appears, click *OK* again to save the change.

✔ Tips

■ While the process is called red eye removal, Photoshop Album will remove any red within the dashed rectangle, so confine the dashed rectangle to just the subject's eyes. In some cases, you may be want to zoom in by 400–800 percent to isolate one eye at a time before applying the effect (**Figure 4.16**).

■ You may need to apply red eye removal several times to get rid of all the red.

■ Many cameras have a red-eye reduction flash, which uses a blinking light to shrink the subject's pupil before firing the main flash. You also can reduce red eye problems by taking pictures at a slight angle to your subject's eyes.

REMOVING RED EYE

Calibrating Your Monitor

Before you begin correcting the brightness, contrast and color of your photos, you need to make sure your computer monitor is calibrated to accurately display photos. You can only calibrate a monitor with a CRT (a cathode ray tube, much like that of a television). LCD monitors (the Liquid Crystal Displays in laptops and thin desktop monitors) cannot be calibrated accurately since your angle of view changes their apparent brightness and color. While calibrating takes a little time, it will make it much easier to produce prints that match what you see onscreen.

To calibrate a CRT monitor:

1. Make sure your CRT monitor has been on for at least 30 minutes, then from the start menu choose Settings > Control Panel > Display. When the Display Properties dialog box appears, click the *Settings* tab and make sure that the *Colors* or *Color quality* panel is set to *High Color (16 bit)*, *True Color (24 bit)*, or *Highest (32 bit)* (**Figure 4.17**). Click *OK* to close the dialog box.

2. Within the Control Panel folder, start Adobe Gamma (**Figure 4.18**). When the Adobe Gamma dialog box appears, choose *Step By Step (Wizard)* and click *Next* (**Figure 4.19**).

3. The Adobe Gamma step-by-step guide will walk you through a series of dialog boxes to check your monitor's brightness, contrast, and color balance (white point). When you're done, the guide will ask you to save the settings as a file, which Photoshop Album will use as its reference point (**Figure 4.20**).

✔ Tip

■ Many monitors now are self-calibrating, making this step unnecessary. Check your display's manual to make sure.

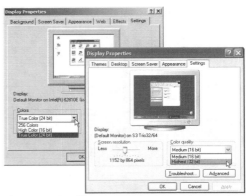

Figure 4.17 To calibrate a CRT monitor, make sure the *Colors* or *Color quality* panel is set to *High Color (16 bit)*, *True Color (24 bit)*, or *Highest (32 bit)*.

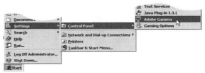

Figure 4.18 Look inside the Control Panel folder to start Adobe Gamma.

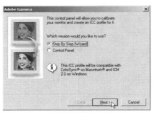

Figure 4.19 When the Adobe Gamma dialog box appears, choose *Step By Step (Wizard)*.

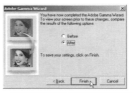

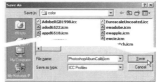

Figure 4.20 The Adobe Gamma program (top) asks you to save the settings (bottom), which Photoshop Album will use as its reference.

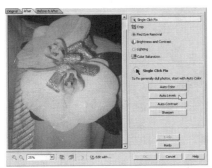

Figure 4.21 To correct the underlit white orchid, *Auto Levels* is applied in the *Single Click Fix* panel.

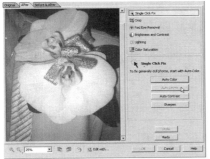

Figure 4.22 After applying *Auto Levels*, the orchid's exposure is much better balanced.

Choose One, Not All Three

In general, using more than one of the three main buttons (*Auto Color, Auto Levels,* or *Auto Contrast*) will wind up making the photo worse rather than better.

Auto Color: Use if a photo seems pale and washed out (undersaturated) or garishly vivid (oversaturated).

Auto Levels: Use if a photo seems dull with not enough difference between the lightest and darkest areas.

Auto Contrast: Less subtle than Auto Levels, this also increases the apparent light-to-dark range of a photo by lightening light areas and darkening darker areas.

Using the Single Click Fix

Photoshop Album includes a powerful feature called Single Click Fix, which lets you quickly correct a photo's color balance, contrast, and focus with a minimum of fuss. If you are using a monitor with a CRT, make sure to calibrate the monitor first (see previous page). Even with a calibrated monitor, a photo that looks great onscreen sometimes may prove disappointing once printed. Pay attention to your prints and you'll gain the experience needed to accurately judge what works best.

To use the Single Click Fix:

1. Select the photo with problems and open the Fix Photo dialog box. By default, *Single Click Fix* is already selected in the upper-right of the dialog box (**Figure 4.21**).

2. Within the Single Click Fix options panel in the lower-right of the dialog box, click *one* of these choices: *Auto Color, Auto Levels,* or *Auto Contrast,* depending on the problem you're trying to solve. In **Figure 4.21**, the white orchid is underlit so *Auto Levels* is used to make the white areas brighter (**Figure 4.22**).

✔ Tips

■ Thanks to the *Undo* and *Redo* buttons, you can feel free to experiment to see which of the three auto buttons (*Auto Color, Auto Levels,* or *Auto Contrast*) works best for a particular photo. With practice, you'll quickly get a sense of which works best for particular photo problems.

■ Once you find which of the three auto buttons works best for a particular photo, you still can use *Sharpen* to further improve the photo's focus. But be careful not to overapply the effect, or your photos may look grainy.

Manually Adjusting Photos

Sometimes the Single Click Fix will not fix a photo as much as you'd like, and manually adjusting a photo may give you better results. Just remember: Even small changes using the controls can have a big effect on a photo's appearance, so apply the effects in tiny steps until you gain experience. As with the Single Click Fix, all your editing takes place in the *After* tab view of the Fix Photo dialog box.

To manually adjust brightness and contrast:

1. Select the photo with problems and open the Fix Photo dialog box, and click *Brightness and Contrast* in the upper-right of the dialog box (**Figure 4.23**).

2. Drag the *Brightness* and/or *Contrast* sliders (**Figure 4.24**). Because Photoshop Album has no live preview, you'll have to wait a moment for the adjustments to be applied to the photo. Toggle between the *Before* and *After* tabs to evaluate your adjustments (**Figure 4.25**).

3. To make other fixes, leave the dialog box open, otherwise click *OK,* and click *OK* again to save the change.

✔ Tip

■ Brightness and contrast adjustments are applied across the entire photo, instead of just problem areas. However, it can still be effective if the main focus of the photo is too bright (left, **Figure 4.25**). In the adjusted photo (right, **Figure 4.25**) the lid of the espresso pot is less washed out. While the stove top has lost detail by becoming darker, it doesn't really matter since it's not the photo's real subject.

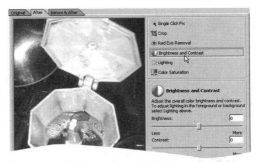

Figure 4.23 Start your manual adjustment by clicking *Brightness and Contrast* in the upper-right of the Fix Photo dialog box.

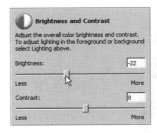

Figure 4.24 Click and drag the *Brightness* and/or *Contrast* sliders to apply the changes to the selected photo.

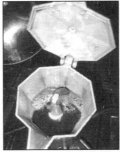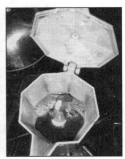

Figure 4.25 To evaluate your adjustments, toggle between the *Before* (top) and *After* (bottom) tab views.

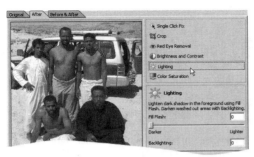

Figure 4.26 Start the manual adjustment by clicking *Lighting* in the upper-right of the Fix Photo dialog box.

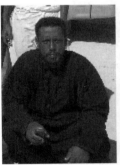

Figure 4.27 Click and drag the *Fill Flash* and/or *Backlighting* sliders to apply the changes to the selected photo.

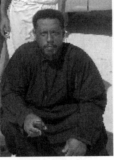

Figure 4.28 Little detail appears in the black shirt (left) before the Fill Flash adjustment (right).

To manually adjust lighting:

1. Select the photo with problems and open the Fix Photo dialog box, and click *Lighting* in the upper-right of the dialog box (**Figure 4.26**).

2. Click and drag the *Fill Flash* and/or *Backlighting* sliders (**Figure 4.27**). Because there's no "preview" feature, you'll have to wait a moment for the adjustments to be applied to the photo in the left-hand pane of the dialog box. You also may want to toggle between the *Before* and *After* tabs to evaluate your adjustments (**Figure 4.28**).

3. If you plan to make other fixes to the photo, leave the dialog box open, otherwise click *OK* and when the Fix Photo alert dialog box appears, click *OK* again to save the change.

✔ Tip

■ Manually adjusting lighting can be particularly effective in an already contrasty photo where details cannot be seen in the brightest or darkest areas. In **Figure 4.28** for example, before the adjustment (left) there was little detail visible in the man's black shirt. After adjustments with the Fill Flash slider, which acts like a flash to bring out foreground details, details can be seen in the shirt while the bright sand in the background has not been washed out (right).

MANUALLY ADJUSTING LIGHTING

To manually adjust color saturation:

1. Select the photo with problems and open the Fix Photo dialog box, and click *Color Saturation* in the upper-right of the dialog box (**Figure 4.29**).

2. Click and drag the *Saturation* slider (**Figure 4.30**). Because there's no "preview" feature, you'll have to wait a moment for the adjustments to be applied to the photo in the left-hand pane of the dialog box. You may need to toggle between the Before and After tabs to judge your adjustments (**Figure 4.31**).

3. If you plan to make other fixes to the photo, leave the dialog box open, otherwise click *OK* and when the Fix Photo alert dialog box appears, click *OK* again to save the change.

✔ Tip

■ Manually adjust saturation when a photo's original colors are so intense that they do not look quite real (**Figure 4.31**).

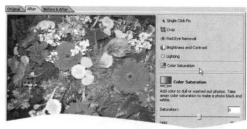

Figure 4.29 Start the manual adjustment by clicking *Color Saturation* in the upper-right of the Fix Photo dialog box.

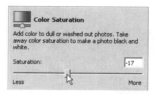

Figure 4.30 Click and drag the *Saturation* slider to change the selected photo.

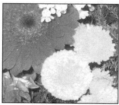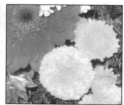

Figure 4.31 While hard to see in black and white, the intense colors in the original (left) have been adjusted to look more realistic (right).

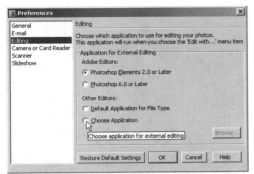

Figure 4.32 To set the external photo editing preference, select *Editing* in the left-hand list and make a choice in the *Application for External Editing* pane.

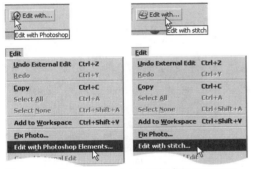

Figure 4.33 Your preferred external editing program will appear in the Fix Photo dialog box (top) and the Edit menu (bottom).

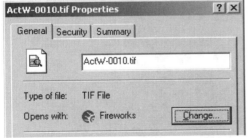

Figure 4.34 The program listed after *Opens with:* is the default application for that file type.

Using Other Photo Edit Programs

By default, Photoshop Album uses Photoshop Elements as its external editing program. Officially priced at $99 and often on sale for less, Photoshop Elements offers all but a few of the professional-level features of Adobe's $600 Photoshop program. You'll find its look and feel familiar after learning Photoshop Album. If you prefer to use another graphics program, it's easy to set that program to launch instead.

To set external editing preference:

1. From the Menu bar, choose Edit > Preferences (Ctrl K).

2. When the Preferences dialog box appears, choose *Editing* in the left-hand list, then use the *Application for External Editing* pane (**Figure 4.32**). By default, *Photoshop Elements 2.0 or Later* is selected. Other choices include *Photoshop 6.0 or later*, the *Default Application* you've already set for a particular file type, or you can select *Choose Application* and use the *Browse* button to navigate to that application.

3. When you've selected the application, click *OK* and its icon will appear in the Fix Photo dialog box (top, **Figure 4.33**) or when you use the Menu bar to choose Edit > Edit with [name of the application] (bottom, **Figure 4.33**).

✔ Tip

■ To see the default application for a particular file type, right-click a file of that type (tif, jpg, or gif for example) and choose Properties from the drop-down menu. Look under the *General* tab, after *Opens with:* (**Figure 4.34**).

To edit with another application:

1. Select the photo you want to fix, open the Fix Photo dialog box, and click the *Edit with* button (**Figure 4.35**).

2. Just before the other editing program opens, you'll see an alert dialog box warning that you cannot make changes in Photoshop Album while the photo is open in the other application. If fact, if you try to switch back to Photoshop Album while the photo is open in the other application, you'll see that the photo is locked (**Figure 4.36**).

3. The external application you selected in *To set the external editing preference* will launch and display the selected photo, where you can then make changes (**Figure 4.37**).

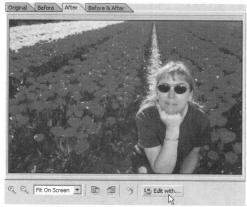

Figure 4.35 To launch your other editing application, click the *Edit with* button in the Fix Photo dialog box.

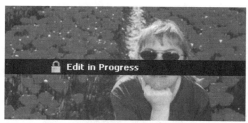

Figure 4.36 Photoshop Album locks the photo as long as you are editing with your other editing application.

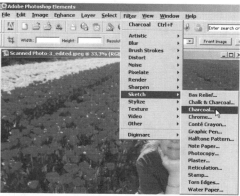

Figure 4.37 The photo opens in Photoshop Elements, where you can make fixes not possible in Photoshop Album.

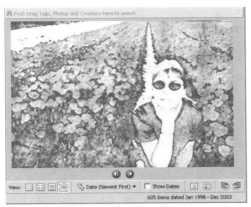

Figure 4.38 Changes made in the other editing program will appear in the Photoshop Album Photo Well.

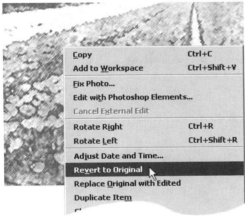

Figure 4.39 If you don't want to save the changes, right-click the photo and choose Revert to Original.

4. When you're done making changes in the external application, save the changes without changing the file's name (see first *Tip* on the next page), and close the photo.

5. Switch back to Photoshop Album and the changes made in the other program will now appear in the Photo Well (**Figure 4.38**). If you don't want to save the changes within Photoshop Album, from the Menu bar, choose Edit > Undo External Editor (Ctrl Z) or right-click the photo and from the drop-down menu choose, Revert to Original (**Figure 4.39**).

(continued on next page)

✔ Tips

- If you are using Photoshop or Photoshop Elements as your external editing program, you can rename the photo in step 4. But if you rename the file using any other editing program, Photoshop Album will not be able to automatically display the changed photo.

- Since keeping track of all your photos is one of the main reasons for using Photoshop Album, make a habit of using Photoshop Album to launch any external editing application, as described above. That way, Photoshop Album will be able to keep straight where all original and edited copies of your photos are stored. If you open a photo directly in another editing application, Photoshop Album will not record the changes and this makes it much more difficult to keep your photos organized.

- If you are using Photoshop or Photoshop Elements as your external editor and choose to rename the photo, when you return to Photoshop Album a Save As dialog box will appear (**Figure 4.40**). Rename the photo, click *Save* and Photoshop Album gives you the choice of saving the file as an edited copy of the original or as a new file. (If you used Photoshop, you'll also have the choice of saving an edited copy in Photoshop's .psd format.) In general, choose to save it as an edited copy of the original file (the default), which will make it easier to find the edited or original photo later on.

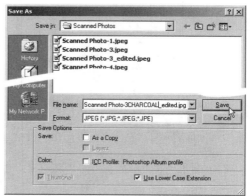

Figure 4.40 If you rename the photo when using Photoshop or Photoshop Elements, a Save As dialog box will appear when you switch back to Photoshop Album.

CREATING PROJECTS

Before digital photography came along, you had three ways to show your photos: as single prints, album collections, or silent slideshows showing one photo at a time. Using your computer and Photoshop Album, those single prints now can be saved in many formats; the albums stored on paper, your hard drive, or a CD; and that slideshow can include background music, professional transitions, and multiple photos onscreen. It's no wonder that digital cameras rank among today's best selling electronic items.

Make sure you have already cropped and edited your photos before diving into creating projects with them. You'll also save time if you add captions to those photos beforehand. By the way, Photoshop Album calls such projects "creations," but I'll just call them projects.

Using the Workspace

The Workspace acts as a digital worktable where you can gather and arrange the photos needed for your project. Once you assemble your photos in the Workspace, the Creations Wizard guides you through turning those photos into a finished project. For more information about the Creations Wizard, see page 89.

Ways to open the Workspace:

◆ In the Shortcuts bar, click the Create icon (top, **Figure 5.1**) and a blank Workspace will appear (**Figure 5.2**).

◆ Click the Show/Hide Workspace icon in the Options bar (bottom, **Figure 5.1**) and a blank Workspace will appear (**Figure 5.2**).

◆ From the Menu bar, choose View > Workspace and a blank Workspace will appear (**Figure 5.2**).

✔ Tips

■ You can resize the Workspace as needed by clicking and dragging its sides or corners.

■ If you have already created and saved a project, you can jump directly to its Workspace by right-clicking the project in the Photo Well and choosing Show Photos in Workspace from the pop-up menu. Or select the project in the Photo Well and click the Show/Hide Workspace icon in the Options bar.

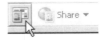
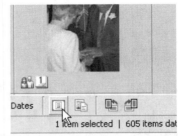

Figure 5.1 To open the Workspace, click the Create icon in the Shortcuts bar (top) or click the Show/Hide Workspace icon in the Options bar (bottom).

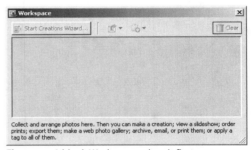

Figure 5.2 A blank Workspace when it first opens.

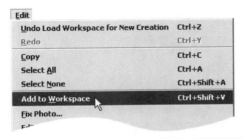

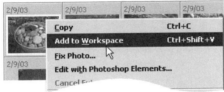

Figure 5.3 To add items to the Workspace, choose Edit > Add to Workspace (top) or right-click any of the photos and choose Add to Workspace (bottom).

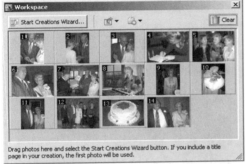

Figure 5.4 The Workspace will open with the selected photos inside.

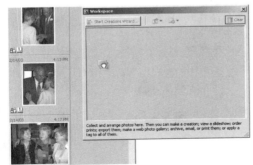

Figure 5.5 You also can click and drag photos from the Photo Well into the Workspace.

Ways to add items to the Workspace:

◆ Select one or more photos in the Photo Well (Shift-click to select adjacent photos; Ctrl-click to select non-adjacent photos), then from the Menu bar, choose Edit > Add to Workspace (Ctrl Shift V) (top, **Figure 5.3**). The Workspace will open with the selected photos inside (**Figure 5.4**).

◆ Select one or more photos in the Photo Well (Shift-click to select adjacent photos; Ctrl-click to select non-adjacent photos), then right-click any of the photos and, from the drop-down menu, choose Add to Workspace (Ctrl Shift V) (bottom, **Figure 5.3**). The Workspace will open with the selected photos inside (**Figure 5.4**).

◆ Open the Workspace, then click and drag photos from the Photo Well into the Workspace (**Figure 5.5**). The photos will appear inside the Workspace.

◆ Select one or more photos in the Photo Well, then open the Workspace using the Workspace icon in the Shortcuts bar. The selected photos will appear inside the Workspace.

◆ Use any of the Photoshop Album find tools (tags, timeline, or calendar view) to display a set of photos in the Photo Well, leave all the items unselected, then open the Workspace, and all those photos will appear inside the Workspace.

✔ Tip

■ If you want to add items to an existing Workspace, do *not* click the Create icon in the Shortcuts bar. Photoshop Album will assume you want to create a *new* Workspace and dump any items already in the Workspace. The photos will not be deleted, of course, but you'll have to start over as far as adding them to the Workspace.

To rearrange Workspace items:

◆ Click on any photo in the Workspace, then hold down your cursor and drag the photo to its new place in the order, and release the cursor (top and middle, **Figure 5.6**). The selected item will appear in its new position (bottom, **Figure 5.6**).

✔ Tip

■ As you drag a photo to its new position, a bright yellow bar will mark the insertion point (middle, **Figure 5.6**).

Ways to remove Workspace items:

◆ Right-click any item in the Workspace and, from the drop-down menu, choose Remove from Workspace (**Figure 5.7**). The item will disappear from the Workspace.

◆ Click and drag any item in the Workspace to the Trash icon in the Workspace toolbar (**Figure 5.8**). Release the cursor over the trash and the item will disappear from the Workspace.

✔ Tip

■ Caution: If you click the Trash icon in the Workspace toolbar, *all* items in the Workspace will be immediately removed. This is so easy to do by mistake that you should use the right-click method unless you really intend to clear the Workspace for a new project.

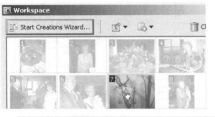

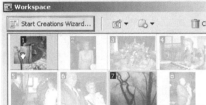

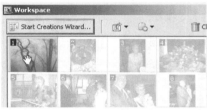

Figure 5.6 To rearrange Workspace items, click and drag any photo to its new place in the order.

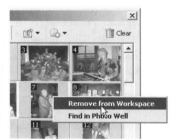

Figure 5.7 To remove Workspace items, right-click any item in the Workspace and choose Remove from Workspace.

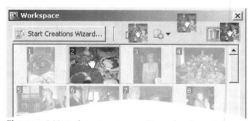

Figure 5.8 You also can remove items by dragging them to the Trash icon in the Workspace toolbar.

REARRANGING, REMOVING WORKSPACE ITEMS

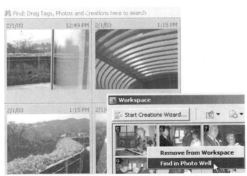

Figure 5.9 To find Workspace items, right-click any photo in the Workspace and choose Find in Photo Well.

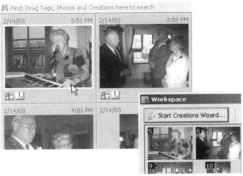

Figure 5.10 Once found, the Workspace photo will be highlighted in the Photo Well.

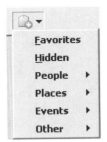

Figure 5.11 To attach tags to Workspace items, select any photo, click the add tag icon, and use the drop-down menu to select a category or sub-category.

Ways to find Workspace photos in the Photo Well:

◆ Right-click any photo in the Workspace and, from the drop-down menu, choose Find in Photo Well (**Figure 5.9**). The photo selected in the Workspace now will appear at the top of the Photo Well surrounded by a bright yellow border (**Figure 5.10**).

◆ Double-click any photo in the Workspace and it will appear in the Photo Well surrounded by a bright yellow border.

✔ Tip

■ This find feature is very useful when you inevitably see a photo in the Workspace that still needs some editing. This lets you jump straight back to the photo in the Photo Well, where you can switch to editing mode and make the needed changes.

To attach tags to Workspace items:

◆ Select any photo or photos in the Workspace, then click the add tag icon and use the drop-down menu to select a category or sub-category you want attached to the photo (**Figure 5.11**). Release the cursor and the tag will be attached to the photo.

✔ Tip

■ This feature can be especially useful if you created some project-related tags ahead of time. That way, as you add photos to a project you are building, you can go ahead and tag those photos, for example, "Wedding Scrapbook" or "Summer Fun Slideshow."

To play an instant slideshow from the Workspace:

◆ Click the Select Command icon in the Workspace toolbar and choose Play Slideshow from the drop-down menu (**Figure 5.12**). A Building slideshow alert box will appear while Photoshop Album assembles the photos into a slideshow. The photos will then appear full-screen. A mini-control panel will appear in the screen's upper right, which you can use to move through or stop the slideshow. Click anywhere on the screen to return to the Photoshop Album Photo Well.

✔ Tips

■ This is what Photoshop Album calls an instant slideshow, which means the sequence is dictated by how the Photo Well is sorted—no matter what the numbers in the Workspace thumbnails might suggest. For more information on sorting the Photo Well, see page 21. If you create a full-fledged slideshow, what Photoshop Album calls a Slideshow Creation, you can control the sequence more precisely (see page 94).

■ As you can see in **Figure 5.12**, the Workspace's Select Command icon gives you direct access to creating any kind of project within Photoshop Album. Once you know how to create such projects (which are explained in the rest of this chapter), this shortcut will save you lots of time.

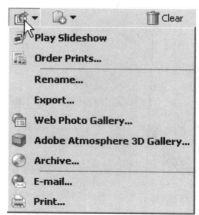

Figure 5.12 To play an instant slideshow of the Workspace photos, choose Play Slideshow from the Select Command icon's drop-down menu.

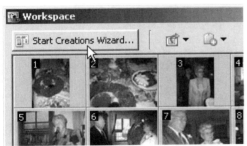

Figure 5.13 After assembling the project photos in the Workspace, click the *Start Creations Wizard* button.

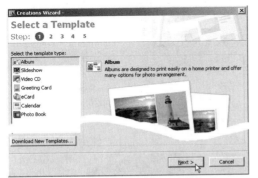

Figure 5.14 When the Creations Wizard dialog box appears, select in the left-hand list the type of project you want to create.

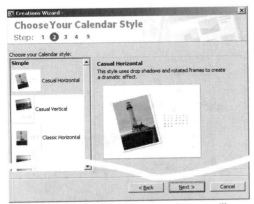

Figure 5.15 The Creations Wizard's style pane will include a variety of choices, with a preview and text description of each.

Using the Creations Wizard

After assembling your project's photos in the Workspace, you use the Creations Wizard to turn them into a finished project. No matter what kind of project you are creating, the Creations Wizard walks you through the same basic steps: picking a project template, selecting its style, customizing the details, previewing the results, and then saving (what Photoshop Album calls publishing) the final project.

To use the Creations Wizard:

1. After assembling the project photos in the Workspace, click the *Start Creations Wizard* button in the upper-left of the Workspace dialog box (**Figure 5.13**). When the Creations Wizard dialog box appears, the *Album* template will be selected by default in the left-hand panel.

2. Within the left-hand panel, select the type of project you want to create and click *Next* (**Figure 5.14**).

3. When the style pane of the Creations Wizard appears, the left-hand style list will include a variety of choices, any one of which you can click to see a preview and a text description in the right-hand panel (**Figure 5.15**). After selecting one you like, click *Next*.

(continued on next page)

4. When the customize pane of the Creations Wizard appears, you'll find lots of ways to tailor your project with such items as titles, headers and footers, message greetings, or even background music. For details on these choices, see the individual projects on pages 92–104. Once you're done customizing the project, click *Next*.

5. When the preview pane of the Creations Wizard appears, the project's title page will be displayed, giving you a chance to check that the right photo, title wording, and layout style are being used. To see the layout and photos for every page, click either the video-style buttons below the first page or the *Full Screen Preview* button in the lower-left corner of the Creations Wizard dialog box (**Figure 5.16**).

6. If during the preview you see something you want to change, you can navigate to the necessary step in the Creations Wizard dialog box by clicking one of the dialog box's *Step* numbers or the *Back* and *Next* buttons (**Figure 5.17**). If you are running a full-screen preview, click the red X in the upper-right of the preview screen (**Figure 5.18**), which will then let you use the *Step* numbers or *Back* and *Next* buttons in the Creations Wizard dialog box.

7. If during the preview you find that some photos are not sequenced properly, click *Rearrange Photos*, found next to the Full Screen Preview button (top, **Figure 5.19**). The Workspace will reappear, where you can reorder your photos (bottom, **Figure 5.19**). Once you finish reordering the photos, click the Workspace's *Back To Wizard* button.

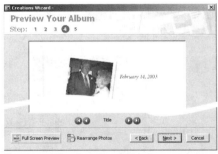

Figure 5.16 The Creations Wizard's preview pane lets you check every project page by clicking the buttons below the first page or by clicking the *Full Screen Preview* button.

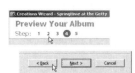

Figure 5.17 Move to any step of the Creations Wizard dialog box by clicking one of the *Step* numbers or the *Back* and *Next* buttons.

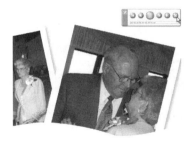

Figure 5.18 Click the red X in the upper-right to close the full-screen preview of your project.

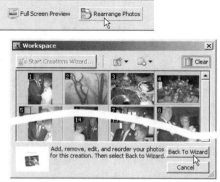

Figure 5.19 If some photos are out of sequence, click *Rearrange Photos* (top) to return to the Workspace. When done, click *Back To Wizard* (bottom).

Using the Creations Wizard

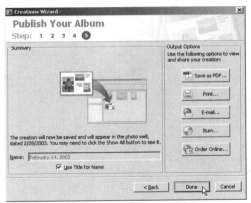

Figure 5.20 When the publish pane of the Creations Wizard dialog box appears, click *Done* to save your project.

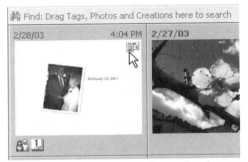

Figure 5.21 The saved project will appear at the top of the Photo Well with a special icon.

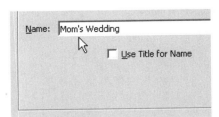

Figure 5.22 To give a project another name, uncheck *Use Title for Name* and type in the *Name* text window.

8. Once you are happy with all the project's elements, click *Next* in the Creations Wizard dialog box.

9. When the publish pane of the Creations Wizard dialog box appears, you can take one of two routes (**Figure 5.20**). If you want to immediately share the project with others, you can click any of the five choices in the *Output Options* panel. But in most cases, you should instead immediately save the project by clicking *Done*, which will place the saved project at the top of the Photo Well (**Figure 5.21**). Once it's saved, you can then share it with others in a variety of forms. For details, see *Sharing Photos* on page 109.

✔ Tips

- Every couple of weeks you may want to click *Download New Templates* in the lower-left corner of the *Select a Template* pane of the Creations Wizard dialog box (**Figure 5.14**) to see if Adobe has added any new templates to the Creations Wizard.

- While you cannot directly select the font used for the titles, captions, and other labels in step 3, different fonts are used in the styles listed in step 2, so take a close look at each style in the right-hand panel preview.

- In step 9, the Creations Wizard by default uses your project's title as the name of the saved project file. If you want to save the project using another, perhaps more descriptive name, uncheck *Use Title for Name* and type your choice in the *Name* text window (**Figure 5.22**).

Creating a Photo Album

Photoshop Album frees you from the tedium of arranging individual photos on pages. There are no sticky corner holders to mess with, no labels to apply, not even acetate sleeves to load. By choosing from a variety of stylish album templates, you can concentrate on using your photos to tell stories and revive memories.

To create a photo album:

1. After adding the desired photos to your Workspace, click the *Start Creations Wizard* button. When the Creations Wizard dialog box appears, select *Album* in the left-hand list, then click *Next*.

2. The left-hand *Album style* list includes a variety of style choices (**Figure 5.23**). Choices selected in the left-hand list are previewed in the right-hand panel. After selecting one you like, click *Next*.

3. When the *Customize Your Album* pane of the Creations Wizard dialog box appears (**Figure 5.24**), you can add a *Title* (which only appears on the album's first page), decide how many photos should appear on each page, whether to *Include Captions* and *Include Page Numbers*, and whether to create a *Header* or *Footer*. The *Photos Per Page* drop-down menu even includes some sequence choices to vary the layout from page to page (**Figure 5.25**). Once you've made your choices, click *Next*.

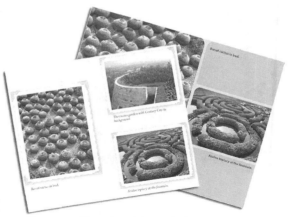

Figure 5.23 Album templates make it easy to create professional-looking projects in a variety of styles.

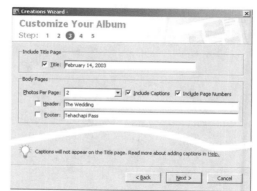

Figure 5.24 Use the *Customize Your Album* pane to add a title, set the number of photos per page, and include captions.

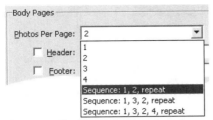

Figure 5.25 The *Photos Per Page* drop-down menu includes choices to vary the layout from page to page.

4. When the *Preview Your Album* pane of the Creations Wizard dialog box appears, the album's title page will be displayed, giving you a chance to check that the right photo, title wording, and layout style are being used. To see the layout and photos for all your album pages, click either the video-style buttons below the first page or the *Full Screen Preview* button in the lower-left corner of the Creations Wizard dialog box.

5. If you want to change something you noticed during the preview, see steps 6 and 7 on page 90.

6. Once you are happy with all the album's elements, click *Next* in the Creations Wizard dialog box.

7. When the *Publish Your Album* pane of the Creations Wizard dialog box appears, save the project by clicking *Done*, which will place the saved project at the top of the Photo Well. Once it's saved, you can then share it with others. For details, see *Sharing Photos* on page 109.

Creating Slideshows

With computer-generated slideshows there's no need for a bulky projector or darkened room. Instead, a sequence of photos can be viewed on your computer screen—or shared with someone else by sending them an email or CD of the slideshow. Photoshop Album helps you set the photo sequence, create transitions between photos at a pace you dictate, and, if you like, add music or spoken audio. You also have the option of watching a slideshow on a TV if you create a Video CD, which can be watched using a DVD player. The growing popularity of DVD players means you may be able to share your slideshow with relatives who don't even own a computer.

To create a slideshow:

1. After adding photos to the Workspace, click the *Start Creations Wizard* button. When the Creations Wizard dialog box appears, select *Slideshow* in the left-hand list and click *Next*.

2. When the *Choose Your Slideshow Style* pane appears, select a style in the left-hand list and click *Next*.

3. When the *Customize Your Slideshow* pane appears, you have various options organized under three panels—*Include Title Page*, *Body Pages*, and *Presentation Options* (**Figure 5.26**). In the *Include Title Page* panel, if you check *Title*, you can type into the text window up to 30 characters for the first photo of your slideshow. The title will replace any existing caption in the slideshow.

4. Use the *Body Pages* panel to set the *Photos Per Page* drop-down menu, which includes choices to vary the number of photos used in each *slide* (the slideshow equivalent of a page) (**Figure 5.25**). If you want to show each photo's existing caption, check *Include Captions*.

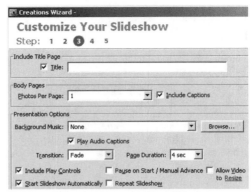

Figure 5.26 Use the *Customize Your Slideshow* pane to set a title, the number of photos per slide, and special effects like background music and transitions.

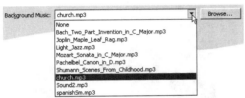

Figure 5.27 The *Background Music* drop-down menu lists recent sound clips and copyright-free music. Or click *Browse* to find other music on your computer.

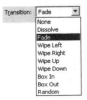

Figure 5.28 The *Transition* drop-down menu lets you control the segue from slide to slide.

5. Use the *Presentation Options* panel to set the *Background Music* played during the slideshow. The drop-down menu includes some copyright-free music, plus any sound clips you've used in other Photoshop Album projects (**Figure 5.27**). To use another sound, click *Browse* to navigate to other music. Or select *Play Audio Captions* if you've already attached remarks or music to the individual photos. Use the *Transition* drop-down menu if you want to smoothly segue from slide to slide (**Figure 5.28**), then use the *Page Duration* drop-down menu to set how many seconds (2, 4, or 10) each slide should appear onscreen. Two seconds is brisk; 10 seconds fits the pace of a lecture.

6. Across the bottom of the *Presentation Options* panel five checkboxes fine-tune the slideshow:

   ▲ **Include Play Controls**. Select if you want the screen to include controls like those in **Figure 5.18**.

   ▲ **Pause on Start/Manual Advance**. Select if you want each slide to stay onscreen until you click to advance.

   ▲ **Allow Video to Resize**. Do not select this unless you are using photos containing at least 5 megapixels, since it will enlarge your photo to fill the screen and may introduce some fuzziness.

   ▲ **Start Slideshow Automatically**. Select to show the first photo at full screen and then show the rest of the slides without prompting.

   ▲ **Repeat Slideshow**. Select for continual display, a good option for an unattended show for passersby.

(continued on next page)

7. Once you've set the customize options, click *Next* at the bottom of the Creations Wizard dialog box to move to the preview pane. When the preview pane appears (**Figure 5.29**), you can see the layout and photos for every slide by clicking the video-style buttons below the first slide or the *Full Screen Preview* button. To change anything in the slideshow, see steps 6 and 7 on page 90.

8. Once you are happy with all the project's settings, click *Next* in the Creations Wizard dialog box, and when the *Publish Your Slideshow* pane appears, click *Done* to save the project. For details on sharing the slideshow, see *Sharing Photos* on page 109.

✔ Tips

■ If you forgot to add captions to some photos before assembling the slideshow, you can still do it: Click the *Rearrange Photos* button when it appears in step 7. When the Workspace appears, right-click any photo, choose Find in Photo Well from the pop-up menu, and then double-click the photo to reach the caption window. Once you've added the caption, click *Back to Wizard* in the Workspace. (See the second tip on page 105.)

■ Feel free to play around with the various transitions in step 5 under the *Customize Your Slideshow* pane (**Figure 5.28**). If you've ever used a program like Microsoft's PowerPoint, you'll recognize such choices as Dissolve or Fade, which are better choices for a slideshow than the distractions of Box In, Box Out, or Random.

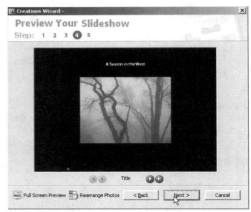

Figure 5.29 Preview the layout by clicking the video-style buttons or the *Full Screen Preview* button.

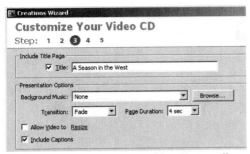

Figure 5.30 The *Customize Your Video CD* pane offers choices that mix features found in photo albums and slideshows.

To create a slideshow on a video CD:

1. Follow steps 1 and 2 of *To create a slideshow* on page 94.

2. When the *Customize Your Video CD* pane of the Creations Wizard appears (**Figure 5.30**), if you check *Title* in the *Include Title Page* panel, you can type into the text window up to 30 characters that will appear with the first photo of your slideshow. Use the *Presentation Options* panel to set the *Background Music* that will be played during the slideshow. For details, see step 5 of *To create a slideshow* on page 95. When you've set the custom settings, click *Next*.

3. Once you've set the customize options, click *Next* at the bottom of the Creations Wizard dialog box to move to the preview pane. When the preview pane of the Creations Wizard appears, you can see the layout and photos for every page by clicking the video-style buttons below the first page or the *Full Screen Preview* button. If you want to change anything in the slideshow, see steps 6 and 7 of *To use the Creations Wizard* on page 90.

4. Once you are happy with all the project's settings, click *Next* in the Creations Wizard dialog box, and when the *Publish Your Video CD* pane appears, click *Done* to save the project. For details on sharing the slideshow by burning a CD, see *Sharing Photos* on page 109.

CREATING A SLIDESHOW ON A VIDEO CD

Creating Greeting Cards and eCards

The Creations Wizard shows you how to create two types of cards: traditional print greeting cards or their digital equivalent, which Photoshop Album calls "eCards," for viewing in email or on a CD. Both types of cards only use the first photo in your Workspace, no matter how many you've added to the Workspace.

To create a greeting card:

1. Add a single photo to the Workspace, click Start Creations Wizard, and then use the Creations Wizard to choose *Greeting Card* (**Figure 5.14**). Click *Next* to choose a card style and click *Next* again to reach the *Customize Your Greeting Card* pane of the Creations Wizard dialog box. (For details, see steps 1–3 of *To use the Creations Wizard* on page 89.)

2. When the *Customize Your Greeting Card* pane appears (**Figure 5.31**), use the *Title* text window to type up to 30 characters that will appear on the front of the card beside or below the photo. Use the *Greeting* text window to type up to 30 characters that appear at the top inside the card. The *Message* will appear below the greeting text inside the card and can include up to 150 characters. Once you're done, click *Next*.

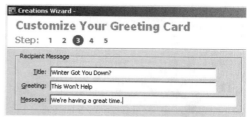

Figure 5.31 The title will appear on the front of the card with the photo, while the greeting and message will appear inside the card.

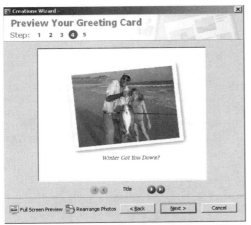

Figure 5.32 The preview pane shows the front of the card. To check the inside, click the forward button or the *Full Screen Preview* button.

3. When the *Preview Your Greeting Card* pane of the Creations Wizard appears, the front of the card will be displayed (**Figure 5.32**). To check the card's inside, click the forward button below the first page or click the *Full Screen Preview*.

4. If you spot something you want to change, navigate to the necessary step in the Creations Wizard dialog box by clicking one of the dialog box's *Step* numbers or the *Back* and *Next* buttons. Once you are happy with all the card's elements, click *Next* in the Creations Wizard dialog box.

5. When the *Publish Your Greeting Card* pane of the Creations Wizard dialog box appears, save the project by clicking *Done*, which will place the saved project at the top of the Photo Well. Once it's saved, you can then print it to share it with others. For details on various printing options, see *Sharing Photos* on page 109.

✔ **Tip**

■ If you have more than one photo in the Workspace, you don't need to remove them. Photoshop Album will use the first photo and ignore the rest.

To create an eCard:

1. Add a single photo to the Workspace, click Start Creations Wizard, and then use the Creations Wizard to choose *eCard* (**Figure 5.14**). Click *Next* to choose a card style and click *Next* again to reach the *Customize Your eCard* pane of the Creations Wizard dialog box. (For details, see steps 1–3 of *To use the Creations Wizard* on page 89.)

2. When the *Customize Your eCard* pane appears (**Figure 5.33**), use the *Title* text window to type up to 30 characters that will appear on the front of the card beside or below the photo. Use the *Greeting* text window to type up to 30 characters that appear at the top inside the card. The *Message* will appear below the greeting text inside the card and can include up to 150 characters. Type your name in the *Signature* text window.

3. Use the *Presentation Options* panel to set the *Background Music* that will be played while the card is onscreen. For details on the other choices, see steps 5 and 6 of *To create a slideshow* on page 95. Once you have set the custom settings, click *Next*.

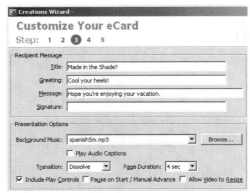

Figure 5.33 The eCard customize choices are similar to those of the printed greeting card.

CREATING AN ECARD

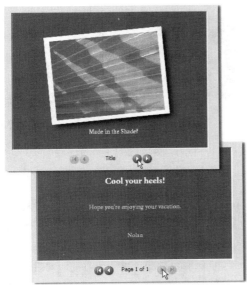

Figure 5.34 The preview pane lets you check your eCard's first screen (top) and second screen (bottom).

4. When the *Preview Your eCard* pane of the Creations Wizard appears, the front of the card will be displayed. To check the card's inside, click the forward button below the first page (**Figure 5.34**) or click the *Full Screen Preview* button.

5. If you spot something you want to change, navigate to the necessary step in the Creations Wizard dialog box by clicking one of the dialog box's *Step* numbers or the *Back* and *Next* buttons. Once you are happy with all the card's elements, click *Next* in the Creations Wizard dialog box.

6. When the *Publish Your eCard* pane of the Creations Wizard dialog box appears, save the project by clicking *Done*, which will place the saved project at the top of the Photo Well. Once it's saved, you can then share it with others. For details, see *Sharing Photos* on page 109.

Creating Photo Calendars

Because they sit out for everyone to see every day, calendars are great for showing off your favorite photos. Unlike store-bought calendars, you can create a calendar for as many, or as few, months as you like. Photoshop Album includes templates for a variety of styles (**Figure 5.35**).

To create a photo calendar:

1. After adding the desired photos to your Workspace, click the *Start Creations Wizard* button. When the Creations Wizard dialog box appears, select *Calendar* in the left-hand list, then click *Next*.

2. Choose a calendar style in the left-hand list, take a look at the preview in the right-hand panel, and once you find one you like, click *Next*.

3. When the *Customize Your Calendar* pane of the Creations Wizard dialog box appears (**Figure 5.36**), you can add a *Title* (which only appears on the calendar's front page without a month) and set the calendar's range using the month and year drop-down menus. Check *Include Captions* if you want them to appear with each month's photo. Once you've made your choices, click *Next*.

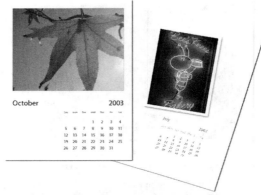

Figure 5.35 Photo calendars can be made in various styles and let you show off your favorite photos.

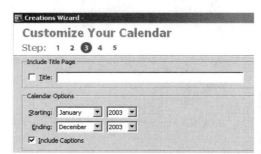

Figure 5.36 Use the customize pane to put a title on the cover, plus set the calendar's time range.

4. When the *Preview Your Calendar* pane of the Creations Wizard appears, the title page of your first month will be displayed. To check the rest of the months, click the forward button below the first page or the *Full Screen Preview* button in the lower-left corner of the Creations Wizard dialog box.

5. If you spot something you want to change, navigate to the necessary step in the Creations Wizard dialog box by clicking one of the dialog box's *Step* numbers or the *Back* and *Next* buttons. Once you are happy with all the months, click *Next* in the Creations Wizard dialog box.

6. When the *Publish Your Calendar* pane of the Creations Wizard dialog box appears, save the project by clicking *Done*, which will place the saved project at the top of the Photo Well. Once it's saved, you can then share it with others. For details on all the choices, which go beyond simply printing it, see *Sharing Photos* on page 109.

CREATING PHOTO CALENDARS

Creating a Bound Photo Book

There's nothing like a bound book to give your digital photos some visual heft. Not only does a professionally bound book look good, it's a sure-fire gift for anyone who doesn't want to sit in front of a computer to see family and friends.

To create a bound photo book:

1. After adding photos to the Workspace, click the *Start Creations Wizard* button. When the Creations Wizard dialog box appears, select *Photo Book* in the left-hand list, then click *Next*.

2. In the *Choose Your Photo Book Style* pane of the Creations Wizard, select a style in the left-hand list to see a preview and text description in the right-hand panel (**Figure 5.37**). After selecting one you like, click *Next*.

3. When the *Customize Your Photo Book* pane of the Creations Wizard appears (**Figure 5.38**), you can add a *Title*, *Subtitle*, and *Author* to appear on the book's cover; a *Header* and *Footer* to appear on every page except the cover; and whether to include captions and page numbers. Once you've made your choices, click *Next*.

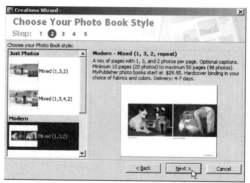

Figure 5.37 The Photo Book style pane of the Creations Wizard dialog box includes a cost estimate for each photo book style, as well as a preview and description of the style.

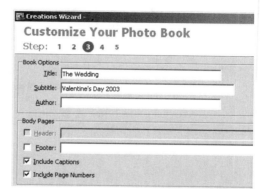

Figure 5.38 Use the customize pane to set the book's title, subtitle, author, headers and footers, page numbers, and captions.

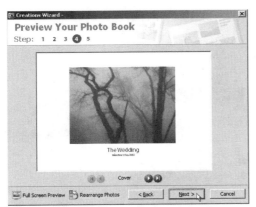

Figure 5.39 Preview the book's layout using the video-style buttons or the *Full Screen Preview* button.

4. When the *Preview Your Photo Book* pane of the Creations Wizard dialog box appears, the book's cover will be displayed, giving you a chance to check that the right photo, title wording, and layout style are being used (**Figure 5.39**). To see the layout and photos for all the book pages, click either the video-style buttons below the first page or click the *Full Screen Preview* button. If you need to change anything, see steps 6 and 7 of *To use the Creations Wizard* on page 90.

5. Once you are happy with the book's design and settings, click *Next* in the Creations Wizard dialog box, and when the *Publish Your Photo Book* pane appears, click *Done* to save the book. For details on getting the book printed, see *Using Online Photo Services* on page 112.

✔ Tips

- Unlike some other projects where the number of photos per page is set in the customize pane, that aspect of photo books is set by the style you choose in step 2.

- You cannot add captions to photos within the Workspace or Creations Wizard. If you set the Photo Well view to single-photo before starting a project, you'll then be able to quickly jump to the Photo Well to add captions as you need them while building a project.

CREATING A BOUND PHOTO BOOK

Finding and Opening Saved Projects

As you create and then save more and more projects, it can become harder to find them amid all the other items in the Photo Well. However, Photoshop Album makes it easy to find them and then open them for viewing or editing.

To find saved projects:

◆ From the Menu bar, choose Find > By Media Type > Creations (**Figure 5.40**). The Photo Well will then display only projects (**Figure 5.41**).

✔ Tips

■ Just as with single photos, you can sort projects by using the rearrangement menu in the Options bar at the bottom of the Photo Well (**Figure 5.41**).

■ To quickly identify individual projects in the Photo Well, open the Properties pane ((Alt)(Enter)) and the name of the selected project will appear in the *Creation Name* text window (**Figure 5.41**).

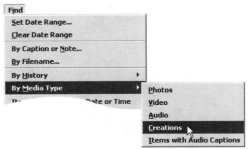

Figure 5.40 To find saved projects, choose Find > By Media Type > Creations.

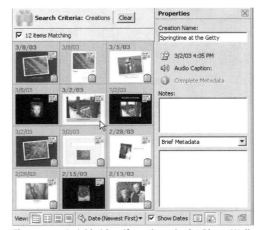

Figure 5.41 Quickly identify projects in the Photo Well by using the Properties pane's *Creation Name* text window.

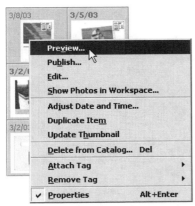

Figure 5.42 To jump to a project's preview window, right-click the photo and choose Preview.

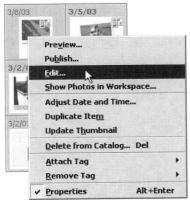

Figure 5.43 To jump to a project's customize window, right-click the photo and choose Edit.

Ways to open saved projects:

◆ Double-click any project in the Photo Well and it will be displayed in the preview pane of the Creations Wizard dialog box. From there you can preview any page or edit the project.

◆ Right-click any project in the Photo Well and from the pop-up menu choose Preview or Edit (**Figures 5.42–5.43**). If you choose Preview, the project will be displayed in the preview pane of the Creations Wizard dialog box. If you choose Edit, the project will be displayed in the customize pane of the Creations Wizard dialog box. From either pane, you then can preview any page or edit the project.

SHARING PHOTOS

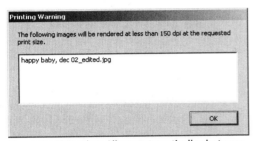

Printing Warning

The following images will be rendered at less than 150 dpi at the requested print size.

happy baby, dec 02_edited.jpg

OK

Figure 6.1 Photoshop Album automatically alerts you if you try to make a print larger than the image will support.

The payoff for all your organizing, editing, and inspired project work comes when you can show off the photos. With Photoshop Album you have lots of ways to do exactly that: print out your own photos or have an online photo service do it; email photos as single shots or sequenced slideshows; or even burn a multimedia CD or DVD.

How Big is Big Enough?

Some digital photographers love to debate the fine points of how to get the best prints. Rather than dive into the nitty gritty of resolution and pixel counts, however, I'll keep it simple: The more pixels captured by the camera, the bigger the print can be and still look sharp. Photoshop Album makes it even simpler: It will automatically display a dialog box to alert you if you attempt to make a print larger than the image will support (**Figure 6.1**).

Such alerts might initially confuse you. A photo looks great on your 17-inch monitor, so why won't it look just as good as an 11-by-14-inch print? The short answer is that monitors use light; printers use dots of ink, which no matter how tiny tend to highlight the fuzziness.

Some rules of thumb: a 2-megapixel camera will produce a sharp 4-by-6-inch print but anything larger will be fuzzy. A 3.2-megapixel camera will produce a decent 5-by-7-inch print and *maybe* an acceptable 8-by-10-inch print. For tack-sharp 8-by-10 prints, use a 4-megapixel or higher camera. As always, there are exceptions: You may be willing to overlook less than perfect results in that favorite low-resolution photo of your nephew.

Finally, check your camera's manual to set the image resolution at its maximum. If you only need to email a photo, Photoshop Album will automatically toss out the extra detail. It's true that you won't be able to store as many images on your memory card. But if you don't capture image detail in the first place, even the most sophisticated software cannot put it back afterward. Considering that memory cards are reusable, they're still cheaper than film, so buy a bigger card or several of them. If you'd like to learn more about the behind-the-scenes details of digital photography, you can visit the Digital Photography Review's nicely illustrated online glossary: www.dpreview.com/learn/.

SHARING PHOTOS

Using Photos on Your Desktop

While it may lack the scope of a big project, using an image of your own for your desktop pattern is a perennially popular way to share photos, even if it's just with your office colleagues. It's so easy to do, you can pick a different photo every day if you like.

To turn a photo into your desktop picture:

1. Select in the Photo Well the photo you want to use.

2. From the Menu bar, choose Edit > Set as Desktop Wallpaper or right-click the photo and choose Set as Desktop Wallpaper in the pop-up menu. The selected photo will immediately appear as the background image of your computer's desktop.

✔ Tip

■ You can reset the desktop back to its original pattern by choosing Start > Settings > Control Panel > Display. When the Display or Display Properties dialog box appears, click the *Background* or *Desktop* tab and pick a pattern from the scroll-down list. Click *OK* to close the dialog box.

USING PHOTOS ON YOUR DESKTOP

Using Online Photo Services

The online photo services bundled into Photoshop Album give you quick access to lab-grade photo prints, Web-based photo galleries, and professionally bound photo books. Creating and ordering them is easy, thanks to step-by-step guides built into the program. You can set up accounts with several online photo services or just one. While each online photo service has a slightly different set of steps for placing orders, all guide you through the process. Most of the online photo services offer first-time-user discounts, so you may want to try several and compare the results.

To set up online photo services:

1. Open your computer's connection to the Internet, then from the Photoshop Album menu bar, choose Online Services > Manage Accounts (**Figure 6.2**). A progress bar will briefly appear as the list of current services is downloaded.

2. When the Create or Modify Online Service Accounts dialog box appears, make sure the *Choose a Service* drop-down menu is set to *All Service Types*. Choose a service from the list and click *Select* (**Figure 6.3**).

   A progress bar will briefly appear as you are connected to the selected online photo provider.

   A welcome screen will appear to guide you through setting up an account (**Figure 6.4**).

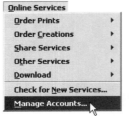

Figure 6.2 To set up online photo services, choose Online Services > Manage Accounts.

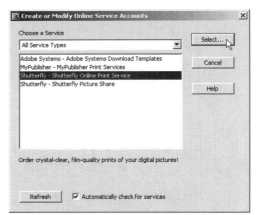

Figure 6.3 Choose a service from the list and click *Select*.

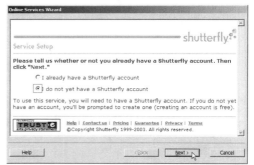

Figure 6.4 A welcome screen will appear to guide you through setting up an online photo service account.

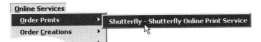

Figure 6.5 Once you have set up an account, you can reach it directly from the Online Services menu.

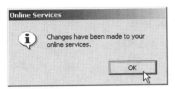

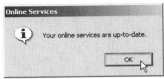

Figure 6.6 Photoshop Album keeps track of new online photo services (top) and when your list is current (bottom).

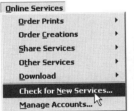

Figure 6.7 You can manually check for new online services by choosing Online Services > Check for New Services.

3. Once you have set up an account, Photoshop Album makes it easy to reach the service directly from the Online Services menu (**Figure 6.5**). If you don't want to order photos just yet, disconnect from the service. You can then either return to step 1 to set up another online photo service or, if you have a dial-up connection, disconnect from the Internet as well.

✔ Tips

- In step 1, if Adobe has added new online photo providers since you last used the online services, an alert dialog box will appear (top, **Figure 6.6**). Any new service will be listed in the Create or Modify Online Service Accounts dialog box, where you can select it as described in step 2.

- You can manually check for new online services anytime by choosing Online Services > Check for New Services (**Figure 6.7**). A dialog box will appear telling you either that new services have been added or that your services are current (**Figure 6.6**).

Emailing Photos and Projects

If you have ever emailed photos to friends or relatives, you probably wrestled with one of the bedeviling details of digital photos: do you send the original or create a fast-to-download version? Do you give the smaller version another name or modify the existing name to signify that it's an email version? How do you keep track of both versions? Again, Photoshop Album makes this sort of problem disappear by handling the naming and tracking behind the scenes.

While you can always manually enter an email address for any photo you're sending out, the contact book offers an easier option. Using it, you can create a list of email contacts, which you can tap whenever you email photos. You can even use the contact book to create groups of contacts interested in particular photos. You can, for example, create a group of your softball teammates, to whom you can easily send photos of the last game. You do not have to think of these groups ahead of time; Photoshop Album lets you create groups as you need them. Photoshop Album also automatically keeps track of which photos you have sent to different people.

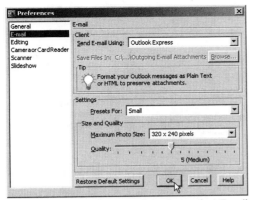

Figure 6.8 In the Preferences dialog box, select *E-mail* in the left-hand list and the *E-mail* panel will appear on the right.

To set email preferences:

1. From the Menu bar, choose Edit > Preferences. When the Preferences dialog box appears, select *E-mail* in the left-hand list and the *E-mail* panel will appear on the right (**Figure 6.8**).

2. Your default email program will be listed in the *Send E-mail Using* text window. If you want to use another program, click *Browse* and navigate to it.

3. In the Settings section, use the *Presets For* drop-down menu to choose the default size you want to use when sending photos. Your choice will automatically change the settings in the *Size and Quality* section, but you can adjust these defaults using the *Maximum Photo Size* drop-down menu and the *Quality* slider (left for poorer quality, right for higher). When you are satisfied with the settings, click *OK* to close the Preferences dialog box.

✔ Tips

- These settings will be used automatically when you email a photo. But you can reopen the Preferences dialog box to change them whenever you have a particular set of photos you want emailed at a different size and quality.

- If you use AOL for sending email, log on to AOL and make sure that the email preference under Associations is set to AOL. That will ensure that Photoshop Album automatically uses AOL to email photos.

SETTING EMAIL PREFERENCES

To open the contact book:

◆ From the Menu bar, choose View > Contact Book ([Ctrl][Alt][B]) (**Figure 6.9**). The contact book will appear, floating on top of the Photo Well.

To add contacts to the contact book:

1. Open the contact book and click *New Contact* (**Figure 6.10**). When the New Contact dialog box appears, fill in the fields you need (you don't have to fill in the *Address* tab), and click *OK* (**Figure 6.11**). The contact book will reappear with the new contact added.

2. You can repeat step 1 to create more contacts, or click *OK* to close the contact book.

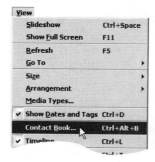

Figure 6.9 To open the contact book, choose View > Contact Book ([Ctrl][Alt][B]).

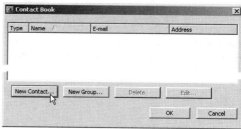

Figure 6.10 To add contacts, click *New Contact*.

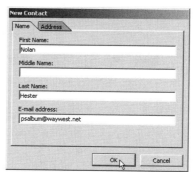

Figure 6.11 Use the New Contact dialog box to add email addresses.

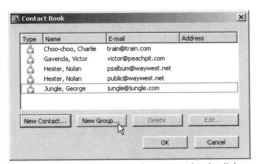

Figure 6.12 To add groups to the contact book, click *New Group*.

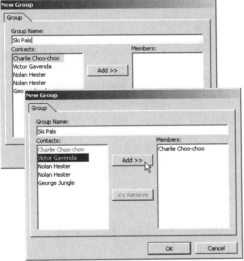

Figure 6.13 Type a name in the *Group Name* text window (top), then click *Add* to build the right-hand *Members* list (bottom).

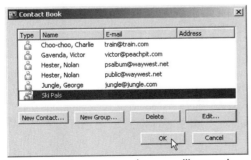

Figure 6.14 New contacts and groups will appear in the expanded contact book.

To add groups to the contact book:

1. Open the contact book and click *New Group* (**Figure 6.12**).

2. When the New Group dialog box appears, type a name into the *Group Name* text window (top, **Figure 6.13**).

3. Select names in the left-hand *Contacts* list, then click *Add* to build the right-hand *Members* list (bottom, **Figure 6.13**).

4. Once you finish adding names to the group, click *OK* to close the dialog box. The contact book will reappear with the new group added (**Figure 6.14**).

To change or delete contacts and groups:

1. Open the contact book, select the contact or group you want to change, and click *Edit* or *Delete*.

2. If you choose *Edit*, when the Edit Contact or Edit Group dialog box appears, make your changes, and click *OK*. The contact book will reappear with the entry updated.

   If you choose *Delete*, when the Confirm Deletion alert dialog box appears, click *OK*. The contact book will reappear with the entry deleted.

ADDING GROUPS, CHANGING, DELETING CONTACTS

To email photos:

1. Select one or more photos in the Photo Well (Shift-click to select adjacent photos; Ctrl-click to select non-adjacent photos).

2. In the Shortcuts bar, click the Share icon, and choose E-mail from the pop-up menu (top, **Figure 6.15**). Or from the Menu bar, choose File > Attach to E-mail (bottom, **Figure 6.15**).

3. A dialog box will appear asking if you want to use the default email application (which you set on page 115). Click *Continue* to close the dialog box and go on.

4. When the Attach Selected Items to E-mail dialog box appears, the photo(s) will be displayed in the left-side *Attachments* panel (**Figure 6.16**). Names and groups from your contact book will be listed in the middle *Send To* panel, from which you can select the ones you want to send email to. Or you can click *Add Recipient*, then use the dialog box that appears to manually add a name not already in the contact book (**Figure 6.17**). Click *OK* to close the dialog box and that name will be added to the *Send To* panel.

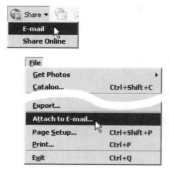

Figure 6.15
To email selected photos, click the Share icon and choose E-mail from the pop-up menu (top), or choose File > Attach to E-mail (bottom).

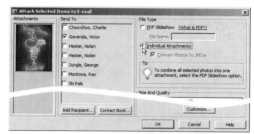

Figure 6.16 The photo to be emailed appears in the left-side *Attachments* panel.

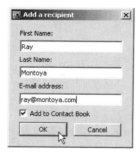

Figure 6.17 Use the *Add a recipient* dialog box to add a name not already in your contact book.

EMAILING PHOTOS

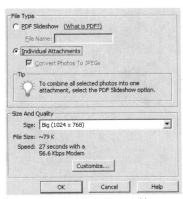

Figure 6.18 The *File Type* panel lets you send the photos as a *PDF Slideshow* or as *Individual Attachments*, which you then adjust in the *Size And Quality* panel.

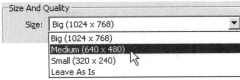

Figure 6.19 Use the *Size* drop-down menu to quickly change the default email settings.

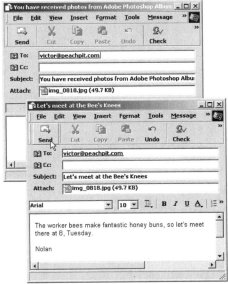

Figure 6.20 Change the default subject line (top) to one of your own, then type in your message, and click *Send* (bottom).

5. The *File Type* panel gives you the choice of sending your photos as a *PDF Slideshow* or as *Individual Attachments* (**Figure 6.18**). (See first *Tip* on page 120 on deciding which to use.) If you select *PDF Slideshow*, identify it in the *File Name* text window. It doesn't need to be the photo's actual file name, just something to help you identify the batch being emailed. While the *Size* text window lists the choice you made when setting your email preferences on page 115), you can change it using the drop-down menu (**Figure 6.19**). Once you've made your choices, click *OK* to close the dialog box.

6. If you chose *Individual Attachments* in step 5, skip to step 7. If you chose *PDF Slideshow* in step 5, a status bar dialog box will appear briefly as the photos are converted to PDF, then an alert dialog box will appear with an estimate of how long it will take with a dial-up connection to upload (and, so, download) the PDF. If you find the time estimate too long to be worth it, click *Cancel*. Otherwise, click *Continue* to close the dialog box.

7. When the email message dialog box appears, it will be addressed to the recipients chosen in step 4 and the photos will be attached (top, **Figure 6.20**). Change the default subject line to one of your own, type in your message, and click *Send* (bottom, **Figure 6.20**).

8. Your email program will launch automatically, make the connection, and send the message and photos. Once the message is sent, you can continue working in Photoshop Album or quit the program.

(tips on next page)

EMAILING PHOTOS

✔ Tips

- The advantage of sending a PDF (Adobe's Portable Document Format), is that it lets you control the order in which the recipient sees your photos. The drawback is that viewing the PDF slideshow requires a special plug-in for Adobe Acrobat Reader. If your recipient doesn't have the plug-in (and I didn't despite being a long-time Acrobat user), they will be guided step-by-step on how to download it from Adobe's Web site. It's pretty easy and only takes a minute, but if your recipient isn't comfortable installing a plug-in, then sending the photos as individual attachments will be less hassle.

- In step 5, besides using the *Size* drop-down menu, you can change the default settings of the selected size for that particular photo by clicking *Customize* (top, **Figure 6.21**). When the preferences dialog box appears (bottom, **Figure 6.21**), drag the *Quality* slider to a new setting and click *OK* to return to the main email dialog box.

- You also can email photos directly from the Workspace by clicking the Select Command icon in the Workspace toolbar and choosing E-mail from the drop-down menu (**Figure 6.22**).

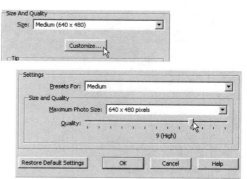

Figure 6.21 Change the default settings for the selected size by clicking *Customize* (top) and then adjusting the *Quality* slider (bottom).

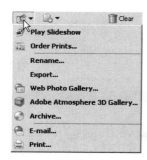

Figure 6.22 Email photos directly from the Workspace by using the Select Command icon in the Workspace toolbar.

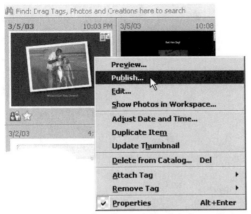

Figure 6.23 To email projects, right-click the project in the Photo Well and from the drop-down menu, choose Publish.

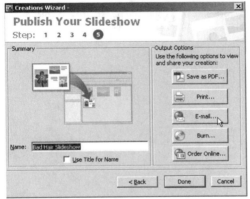

Figure 6.24 In the Creations Wizard dialog box, click *E-mail* in the right-hand *Output Options* panel.

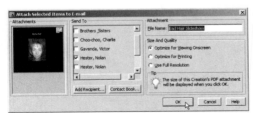

Figure 6.25 Prior to being emailed, the project appears in the left-side *Attachments* panel.

To email projects:

1. Right-click the project in the Photo Well and from the drop-down menu, choose Publish (**Figure 6.23**).

2. When the publish pane of the Creations Wizard dialog box appears, click *E-mail* in the *Output Options* panel (**Figure 6.24**).

3. When the Attach Selected Items to E-mail dialog box appears, the project will be displayed in the left-side *Attachments* panel (**Figure 6.25**). To continue, see step 4 of *To email photos* on page 118.

Printing Photos

When it comes to printing your photos, Photoshop Album offers two different approaches: use your own desktop printer (what Photoshop Album calls local printing) or order prints from an online photo service. Using your own printer means no waiting and Photoshop Album includes some great printing options. The Picture Package, for example, arranges a preset variety of photo sizes on a single page. The results resemble the photo packages school photographers often sell. The advantage of using an online photo service is getting photo lab-quality prints—and not messing with finicky desktop printers.

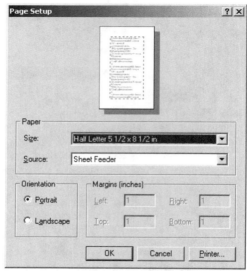

Figure 6.26 Make sure the paper *Size* is correct or change it with the drop-down menu.

To set your printer options:

1. From the Menu bar, choose File > Page Setup (Ctrl Shift P).

2. When the Page Setup dialog box appears, make sure the paper *Size* is set for the photo-quality paper you'll be using or change it with the drop-down menu (**Figure 6.26**). In most cases, the *Source* will not need changing, though you may need to change the *Orientation*.

3. If you have more than one printer (increasingly likely as people buy different printers to handle documents and photos), click *Printer* to make sure you have your photo printer activated. When you return to the Page Setup dialog box, click *OK* to close the dialog box.

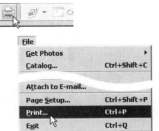

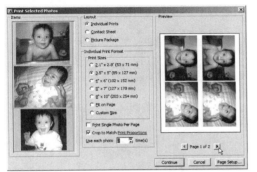

Figure 6.27 To print photos on your own printer, click the Print icon or choose File > Print.

Figure 6.28 Photos to be printed appear in the left-hand panel, options in the center, and a Preview panel on the right.

To print photos on your own printer:

1. In the Photo Well, select the photos or project you want printed. In the Shortcuts bar, click the Print icon or, from the Menu bar, choose File > Print (**Figure 6.27**).

2. If you have selected pictures with too low a resolution to look good printed, a warning dialog box will list their names. If you want the print anyway, click *OK* and proceed. Otherwise, when the Print Selected Photos dialog box appears in step 3, click *Cancel* to return to the Photo Well where you can deselect those photos.

3. When the Print Selected Photos dialog box appears, the selected photos will appear in the left-hand panel (**Figure 6.28**).

(continued on next page)

PRINTING PHOTOS ON YOUR OWN PRINTER

4. In the top-middle *Layout* panel, choose whether you want to print:

▲ **Individual Prints (Figure 6.29)**. If you make this choice, select your *Print Sizes* (you can only choose one), decide if you want to just *Print Single Photo Per Page* (which takes a lot more pages), and whether to *Crop to Match Print Proportions* (try it both ways, using the *Preview* panel to see if the crop cuts out key parts of the photos). Use the arrows in the *Use each photo* text window to set how many prints of each photo you want.

▲ **Contact Sheet (Figure 6.30)**. If you make this choice, use the arrows in the *Columns* text window to control the arrangement of the photos, then select any of the three items in the *Show Photo Properties* panel that you want to appear. If your selections will take more than a single page, you will be able to select *Show Page Numbers* as well.

▲ **Picture Package (Figure 6.31)**. If you make this choice, use the *Layout* drop-down menu to choose your mix of photo sizes.

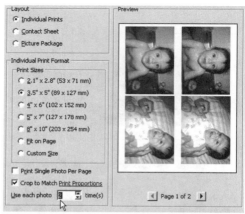

Figure 6.29 The *Individual Prints* options control the size, cropping, and number of copies.

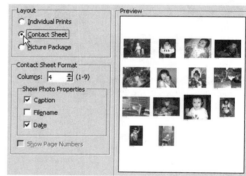

Figure 6.30 The *Contact Sheet* options control the layout and information shown for each photo.

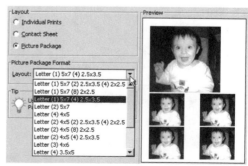

Figure 6.31 The *Picture Package* layout offers different mixes of photo sizes on the same sheet.

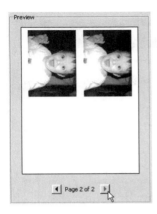

Figure 6.32
The *Preview* panel shows how the photos will be laid out on each page.

5. The right-hand *Preview* panel will show how the photos will be laid out on the pages. If the photos will require more than one page, you can click the forward and back arrows to see previews of all the pages (**Figure 6.32**).

6. Once you have made your choices, click *Continue* in the lower-right of the Print Selected Photos dialog box. The print dialog box for your printer will appear, where you can make further adjustments if needed, and then click *Print*. The dialog box will close, your photos will begin printing, and the Photo Well will reappear.

PRINTING PHOTOS ON YOUR OWN PRINTER

To order prints online:

1. Open your computer's connection to the Internet.

2. In the Photo Well, select the photos or project you want printed, then from the Menu bar, choose Online Services > Order Prints and select an online photo service from the submenu.

3. If this is the first time you've used this service, two dialog boxes will appear. The first explains the terms of using the online services. Click *Agree* to continue. The second dialog box says Adobe is not responsible for any problems with the online photo service providers. Click *OK* to continue.

4. When the Online Services Wizard appears with the welcome screen for the selected online photo service, log in using your account name and password.

5. Follow the onscreen step-by-step instructions, which guide you through such choices as how many prints to order (**Figure 6.33**).

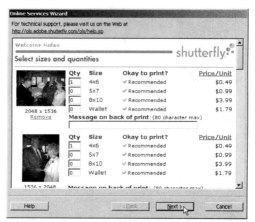

Figure 6.33 Onscreen instructions guide you through such choices as how many prints to order.

6. After filling in the shipping address, other information, and calculating the cost, you'll be asked to upload your photos, which can take a few minutes to several hours, depending on your Internet connection, and the number and size of the photos. Once the upload finishes, you can log out from the online photo service.

✔ Tips

■ In step 2, you have the option of clicking the Order Online icon, choosing an online photo service from the drop-down menu at the bottom of the dialog box that appears, then clicking Select in the Create or Modify Online Services Account dialog box. But why bother? It's much quicker to just use the Menu bar.

■ In step 5, you have the option of ordering prints and having them shipped to another address, which is a great option for sending relatives prints without a bill.

ORDERING PRINTS ONLINE

To order a bound photo book online:

1. Open your computer's connection to the Internet.

2. In the Photo Well, select the photo book project you want printed, then from the Menu bar, choose Online Services > Order Creations and select an online photo service from the submenu (**Figure 6.34**).

3. The photo book will appear in a dialog box that resembles the project Workspace in which you first created it (**Figure 6.35**). The drop-down menu at the bottom of the dialog box already will list the online photo service you picked in step 2, so click *OK*.

4. If this is the first time you've used this service, two dialog boxes will appear. The first explains the terms of using the online services. Click *Agree* to continue. The second dialog box says Adobe is not responsible for any problems with the online photo service providers. Click *OK* to continue.

5. When the Online Services Wizard appears with the welcome screen for the selected online photo service, log in using your account name and password (**Figure 6.36**).

6. Follow the onscreen step-by-step instructions, which are actually simpler than those for ordering prints since you already made most of the format and style choices when creating the book project.

7. After filling in the information fields, you'll be asked to upload (or build) the PDF file of the book, which you created on page 104 (**Figure 6.37**). Once the upload finishes, you can log out from the online photo service.

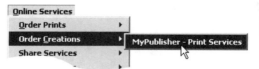

Figure 6.34 To order a bound photo book, choose Online Services > Order Creations and make a choice from the submenu.

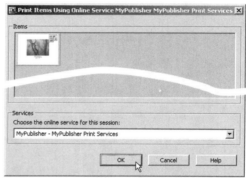

Figure 6.35 The photo book will appear in a dialog box that resembles a project Workspace.

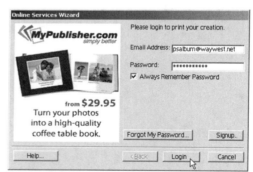

Figure 6.36 Log in when the welcome screen for the photo book printing service appears.

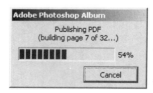

Figure 6.37 A PDF version of the photo book will be created and uploaded during the order process.

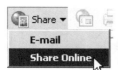

Figure 6.38 To share photos using a Web site, click the Share icon and choose Share Online from the drop-down menu.

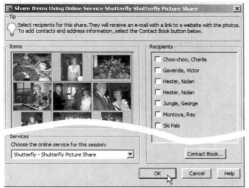

Figure 6.39 The photos will appear in a dialog box, along with a list of your contact book addresses.

Sharing Photos with a Web Site

As more people grow comfortable using the Web for almost anything, an online photo album becomes more appealing. Why wait to download photos and then wait while they print out, when you can just surf over for a peek at the grandchildren's Web photo album? While you could build your own Web site for those photos, most online photo services offer pre-built sites. All you need to do is post the photos and, if you like, assign a password, so that only friends and relatives can reach the site. Send them an email with the Web address and password, and you can get back to taking more photos.

To share photos using a Web site:

1. Make sure you've set up an account with an online photo service that offers Web sharing. (See *To set up online photo services* on page 112.) Open your computer's connection to the Internet.

2. In the Photo Well, select the photos or project you want to share on the Web site.

3. In the Shortcuts bar, click the Share icon and choose Share Online from the drop-down menu (**Figure 6.38**), or from the Menu bar, choose Online Services > Share Services and select an online photo service from the submenu.

4. The photos will appear in a dialog box with a list of your contact book addresses (**Figure 6.39**). Use the *Recipients* panel to select who should receive an email notice about the Web site. Check that the drop-down menu at the bottom of the dialog box lists the online photo service you want to use, and click *OK*.

(continued on next page)

5. If this is the first time you've used this service, two dialog boxes will appear. The first explains the terms of using the online services. Click *Agree* to continue. The second dialog box says Adobe is not responsible for any problems with the online photo service providers. Click *OK* to continue.

6. When the Create or Modify Online Service Accounts dialog box appears, the online photo service chosen in step 5 already will be selected, so click *Select* (top, **Figure 6.40**). A progress bar will appear briefly as you connect to the online photo service (bottom, **Figure 6.40**).

7. When the Online Services Wizard appears with the selected online photo service's welcome screen, log in (**Figure 6.41**). Another progress bar will appear briefly as your user name and password are authenticated.

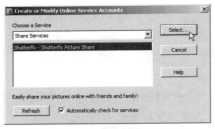

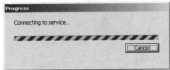

Figure 6.40 The photo service chosen in step 5 already will be selected, so click *Select* (top) and a progress bar will appear briefly as you connect to the service (bottom).

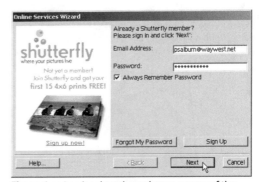

Figure 6.41 Log in when the welcome screen of the online photo service appears.

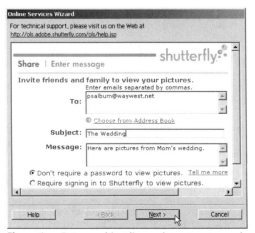

Figure 6.42 Enter a subject line and message to send to everyone being told about the Web site photos.

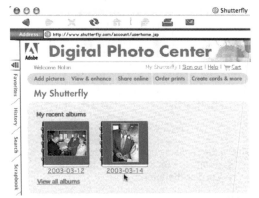

Figure 6.43 Once they receive your message, recipients can log on and see the photos online.

8. A dialog box will appear listing the recipients chosen in step 4, and ask you to enter a subject heading for the email, along with a brief message (**Figure 6.42**). After doing so, the online photo service will upload your photos. That can take a few minutes to several hours, depending on your Internet connection and the number of photos. Once the upload finishes, you can log out from the online photo service. An email will be sent to each recipient with your message and the address of the Web site address where the photos can be seen (**Figure 6.43**).

Saving Photos to CD or DVD

Saving your photos to a CD or DVD is a great way to share them with others. And if you burn a Photoshop Album project, you can preserve the various sequence and title options added to a slideshow, PDF-based album, or other project. If you create the slideshow as a video CD, as explained on page 97, the CD can even be viewed on a DVD player attached to a television.

A less fancy, but just as valuable, way to burn a CD is to store individual photos as an archive. An archive cannot contain Photoshop Album projects, but it does offer a way to store your original photos for safe keeping in another location. An archive also lets you free up space on your hard drive by storing the original images on the disc, while Photoshop Album keeps a much smaller proxy file on your computer. When you attempt to work on the proxy image, Photoshop Album will automatically ask for the archive disc by name.

To burn a project to a CD or DVD:

1. Select your project in the Photo Well, right-click it, and choose Publish from the pop-up menu.

2. When the publish pane of the Creations Wizard appears, click *Burn* in the right-hand *Output Options* panel (**Figure 6.44**).

3. A dialog box will ask you to insert the disc (top, **Figure 6.45**). After doing so, click *OK* and the project will be written to the disc (bottom, **Figure 6.45**).

4. Once the burn is completed, the dialog box will automatically close, and you can eject the disc for labeling.

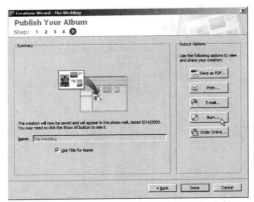

Figure 6.44 To burn a project to a CD or DVD, click *Burn* in the right-hand *Output Options* panel.

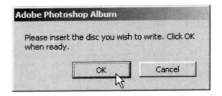

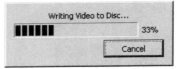

Figure 6.45 A dialog box asks you to insert a disc (top). Click *OK* and the project will be written to disc (bottom).

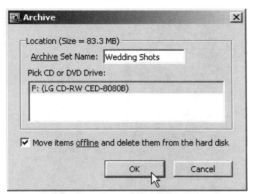

Figure 6.46 The Archive dialog box includes the option of moving items *offline* and deleting the originals from the computer.

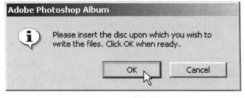

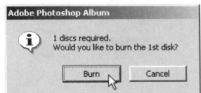

Figure 6.47 A dialog box asks you to insert the disc (top), while another reconfirms that you're ready to *Burn* the disc (bottom).

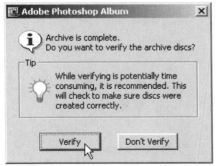

Figure 6.48 Once the disc(s) have been burned, click *Verify* to make sure they can be read.

To archive individual photos to CD or DVD:

1. Select the photos in the Photo Well you want to archive, and from the Menu bar, choose File > Archive.

2. When the Archive dialog box appears, give your archive a *Set Name* and pick a CD or DVD drive for burning the disc(s) (**Figure 6.46**). You also have the option of moving items off your hard drive and deleting the originals from the computer. If you select this option, Photoshop Album will keep proxy images on your computer and prompt you to insert the disc when it needs the originals. Once you have made your choices, click *OK*.

3. A dialog box will appear asking you to insert the disc (top, **Figure 6.47**). Once you do so, click *OK*. Photoshop Album determines how many discs are needed and reconfirms that you're ready to begin (bottom, **Figure 6.47**). Click *Burn* to start.

4. A progress bar will track the archiving. Another dialog box will alert you when the burn is finished and remind you to label the completed disc. Click *OK* to continue. If the archive requires multiple discs, you will be prompted to insert the next disc.

5. Once the disc(s) have been burned, you'll be asked if you want to verify that the disc was burned properly (**Figure 6.48**). Click *Verify* and follow the dialog box prompts to test the disc(s). Once the testing is complete, click *OK* to close the dialog box.

ARCHIVING INDIVIDUAL PHOTOS TO CD OR DVD

Exporting Photos

If you want to reformat a group of photos to work with them in another program that, perhaps, only handles PNG files, you'll need to export them. You cannot export Photoshop Album projects but anything else can be easily reformatted. To decide what file format to export in, check the requirements of the other program you'll be using. For a quick look at the differences between JPEG and TIFF files, see *A Tale of Two Formats* on page 8.

To export photos:

1. Select the photos in the Photo Well you want to export, and from the Menu bar, choose File > Export.

2. When the Export dialog box appears, choose a *File Type* based on the needs of the program you'll be using to import the images (**Figure 6.49**). Use the *Photo Size* drop-down menu to choose what size the exported photo should be (**Figure 6.50**). If you choose *JPEG* as your format, use the *Quality* slider to set the level of detail retained (higher is better).

3. In the *Location* panel, click *Browse* and navigate to where you want the exported photos stored. Use the *Filenames* panel to either keep the original name or create a *Common Base Name*, from which sequentially numbered file names will be generated.

4. Once you have chosen your settings, click *Export*. A progress bar will appear briefly, then a dialog box confirming the export will appear. Click *OK* and you will be returned to the Photo Well.

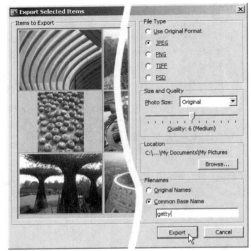

Figure 6.49 Choose a *File Type* based on the needs of the program where you'll be using the images.

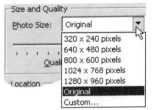

Figure 6.50 Use the Export dialog box's *Photo Size* drop-down menu to choose the size for the exported photo(s).

INDEX

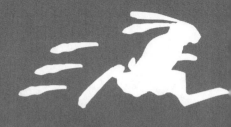
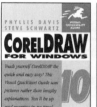 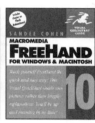 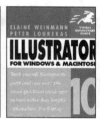 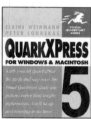 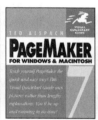 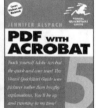

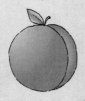

WWW.PEACHPIT.COM

Quality How-to Computer Books

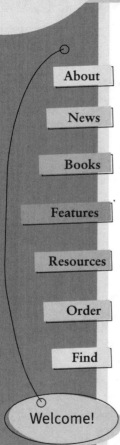

- About
- News
- Books
- Features
- Resources
- Order
- Find

Welcome!

Visit Peachpit Press on the Web at www.peachpit.com

- Check out new feature articles each Monday: excerpts, interviews, tips, and plenty of how-tos

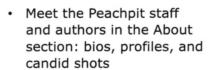

- Find any Peachpit book by title, series, author, or topic on the Books page

- See what our authors are up to on the News page: signings, chats, appearances, and more

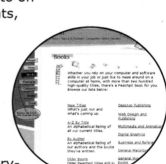

- Meet the Peachpit staff and authors in the About section: bios, profiles, and candid shots

- Use Resources to reach our academic, sales, customer service, and tech support areas and find out how to become a Peachpit author

Peachpit.com is also the place to:

- Chat with our authors online
- Take advantage of special Web-only offers
- Get the latest info on new books